Life is nothing more than a dog race.
Maddog McDermutt

Once around is all you get.
Fleas Finnegan

It's that first turn that gets you.
Hugh Mungas

No photo finishes in this lifetime.
Little Elsie

Wolves? There are no wolves in Montana.
Bill Eagleberry

There are several ways to mount a dog.
Worthington, Sr.

Sometimes I wonder about public education.
Dr. Mayonaisse

DOWN UNDER JONES

by

ROBERT SCOTT MCKINNON

Illustrations and cover by
TOM QUINN

Text copyright © Robert Scott McKinnon
Illustrations copyright © Tom Quinn
All rights reserved by Robert Scott McKinnon

Library of Congress Catalog Card Number: 2001 131379

Library of Congress Cataloging in Publication Data
McKinnon, Robert Scott
Down Under Jones

Summary: First year junior high English teacher Ryan McNulty meets track dropout Jones, an Australian Greyhound import, and agrees to give the dog a home, to the astonishment of his wife and fellow teachers. Torn between teaching and dog racing, the narrator is convinced his track reject can run. The need to prove his dog's true speed drags the narrator into one crazy adventure after another, from Montana to Florida to South Dakota.

1. Dogs—fiction. 2. Greyhound adoption—fiction. 3. Dog racing—fiction. 4. Montana—fiction. 5. Education—satire.

Published by

IOWA GREYHOUND ASSOCIATION
Underwood, Iowa

ISBN 0-9651943-1-0

DOWN

UNDER

JONES

by

ROBERT SCOTT MCKINNON

Illustrated by

TOM QUINN

PREFACE

I recognized the yellow, wrinkled-up sheets of paper the moment I saw them.

They had been under my bottom slide-out drawer, under the heavy duty reference books I never used, all these years.

I hesitated, then I carefully plucked them out, set them on the desk, sat down, took a deep breath.

I leaned back in my chair, looked them over. How many years? Thirty?

Thirty years ago, Maddog McDermutt had read this letter to me, and the rest of my fellow dog trainers, on the tarmac at the Rapid City, South Dakota, Black Hills Greyhound Park. I slipped my reading glasses on my nose.

Thirty years ago Maddog McDermutt's deep, scratchy voice with a slight Scotch accent, boomed out the welcome news from Fard Worthington.

Dear Maddog:

Sorry we did not make Rapid City for opening night. I am writing this note from an island on the Missouri where we have been hiding out. I have taken the opportunity to work with the dogs daily. I plan to float the Missouri River to Fort Peck, then drive the team to Rapid, by back roads and cross country. I shall call you when I can. Looking forward to seeing you all.

Fard Worthington.

P.S. Tell Mr. McNulty Jones is fine. He is our lead dog. He'll get us there.

Sheldon and Harry stuck their noses in the door. "Hey!" Sheldon said, "they're down the hall in 215, waiting to give you your gold watch."

"With something very sinful to eat," Harry added.

I nodded. "You guys remember that day you showed up at Rapid City to watch Jones run?"

"Sure," Sheldon said.

"Who could forget that?" Harry said.

I held up Fard's letters. "I ran across Fard's letters, cleaning out my desk." I cleared my throat, said, "They kind of took my breath away. Why don't you go on. I'd like to have a moment, then put them away in a safe place."

"Sure, OK," Sheldon said. "We'll tell everybody to hang on for a couple of minutes."

"You're retiring," Harry said. "Take all the time you want. I'll just have a bigger helping of ice cream and cake."

I nodded, stared at the second letter. The farewells from the kids were bad enough; the faculty party in 215 I would survive. A flood of memories exploded in my brain: I wiped my cheeks and eyes with a sleeve. And I could see him again, that knot-headed Australian who changed my life forever: Down Under Jones.

I set my elbows on the desk, rested my chin in my hands, stared at the blank blackboard at the back of the room. My retirement party down the hall could wait.

Thirty years ago came at me with a rush.

ONE

Monday. Thank heavens for Third Period prep. I dropped my load of books and papers on the faculty room desk with a thud. The principal's ash tray bounced, ashes settling around and on my students' papers. I took a deep breath, blew the ashes off, and away; I flicked the principal's cigi-butt into the garbage can in the corner.

Bull's-eye!

"Hey, give that man two points," Harry Ringling, one of our math teachers said, shuffling into the room. "The man is hot, he made the shot. Gimme five, man." And he pounded rhythmically on the table.

I poured myself a cup of coffee, loaded the awful stuff up with sugar and cream, stirred. Smelled like battery acid. At least it was hot. I sat down, wondering what to attack first. I had 180 spelling papers, 180 two-page compositions, more than a week's worth of grammar workbook exercises, and various "activity" exercises related to our literature book. In addition to all of that I had forms to fill out on several children, as to why.....that could be anybody's guess; and I had to turn in my goal for the year, to the principal, who rumor had it would be observing my teaching methods and lesson plans in the very near future.

Sheldon Adamson, the orchestra teacher, came in, right on schedule, put a beat-up violin case on the table, poured himself a cup of coffee.

I looked over at the two of them from behind my pile of papers. "There must be a storm coming," I said. "Tremendous barometric pressure. I've never seen the kids so squirrelly."

Sheldon studied my mountain of books and papers, seated himself, then said, "Surely you don't read all that stuff."

"I don't know what I'm doing," I said. "I'm floundering. I just don't get it. I have 180 students, not counting homeroom, hall duty, lunch duty, and tutoring. How do you guys do it? You never seem to have any outside work."

Sheldon shrugged, tapped on the violin case. "I teach orchestra," he said. "I don't do papers."

Harry said, "My students exchange papers for correction."

I said, "I do that with spelling from time to time. But just recording the spelling grades takes a lot of time."

"So don't record," Sheldon said.

"Take a fifty word spelling examination every Friday just for fun?"

"Don't record."

"OK," I said. "Take that faculty meeting last night, lasted until six. It took that fool principal of ours two hours to explain goals?"

"Goals are important," Sheldon said. "We have to have goals. Realistic goals. I spend thirty-five percent of my waking hours pondering goals."

Harry grinned.

I nodded, pulled out a piece of paper. Harry and Sheldon watched intently as I sketched.

"What's that?" Harry asked.

I drew a football field, the ten yard lines, the end zones, the goal posts. I circled one of the goal posts.

"That," I said, "is my goal."

"I love it," Harry said.

Sheldon nodded. "You would have made a fine football coach."

"Did I ever tell you guys I flunked Methods?"

"That's impossible," Harry said

"I had to take it over."

"And?"

I sipped my battery acid. "I got a D."

"There's hope for you yet," Sheldon said.

A counselor, female gender, came in. I didn't know her name. I also didn't know what counselors do. I think she talked to kids from time to time. Once in awhile I would see her around, but I never came to know her, in that she didn't participate in hall duty, or lunch duty, or locker duty, or outside duty. She stood at the end of the table, arms crossed, somewhat melancholy I thought.

She spoke to Sheldon: "Are you the one who sent Arnold Barnes down to metal shop for a left-handed monkey wrench?"

Harry brightened right up. "Did he find one?"

"Not funny," the counselor said, shaking her head thoughtfully. "Especially when he comes back with a note looking for striped paint."

I couldn't help myself. I had to grin.

"While you find all that so amusing, Mr. First Year Teacher, I might add that the administration of Paris Gibson Junior High has received three calls, on your selection of reading materials, something about a bum blowing out the brains of an overgrown man with a learning disability and killing puppies and mice and a woman and an old smelly dog."

"That'd be John Steinbeck's <u>Of Mice and Men</u>," I said. "Lenny was going to get shot anyway. Or worse."

The counselor sucked air, gasped, then spoke from behind a cupped hand. "And crushing a puppy? Reading that to ninth graders?"

"Squish," Harry said, clenching his fist.

"Sounds like a great book," Sheldon said.

I added the clincher: "John Steinbeck's <u>Of Mice and Men</u> is on this school district's ninth grade reading list."

Sheldon and Harry smirked, as though victory was mine.

The counselor made a note on her clipboard. "*Was*. The book *was* on this school district's reading list." She turned, marched out the room.

"What's her problem?" I asked.

"Nothing," Sheldon said. "She's administrative timber."

"Don't let that stuff get you down," Harry said. "Just remember that these kids really do appreciate you. Word gets around. You're OK. Kids say you're a little uptight, but OK."

"How generous," I muttered.

"One kid that we share," Sheldon said, "was complaining about your jokes. Said your jokes stink. Said you were a great teacher but don't try to be a comedian."

Harry jumped right in, cut me off: "You know what you need, speaking of squishing dogs, McNulty, is a dog. You need a dog."

"A dog?"

"A dog."

Sheldon put both hands on his violin case, leaned forward. "Every teacher should have a dog. A good dog. Your wife and kids, if you ever have any kids, will never understand you and your career. But your dog might. We all have dogs. I have an Irish setter. Harry has a black lab. After a hard day, you go home, your dog greets you, loyal, friendly, happy to see you, in his way thanking you for the sacrifices, for putting up with the dunderheads down here, including that counselor. Man's best friend, you know, is the dog. A teacher's best friend is a dog. I think every teacher in this school has a dog. Old Spencer, he has a weener dog."

Harry nodded. "And Bradley has a Saint Bernard. Big sucker. You gotta get a dog."

"Even old lady Pintsrube in 283 has two poodles. Those poodles are her salvation. Because of those two poodles, she's going to make retirement this year."

I said, "You haven't mentioned that counselor.... what's-her-name.... she have a dog?"

"Are you kidding?" Harry said

"It's fairly evident," Sheldon said, tapping on his violin case, "that she does not."

"What's with the violin?" I asked.

"Oh, I took it away from a kid," Sheldon said. "The second violin section was having a dual with the viola players, using the instruments as shields, the bows as swords."

The bell rang for fourth period.

13

TWO

Three weeks later on a school night Harry and Sheldon picked me up for a night at the dog races. They'd been after me for some time.

"We'll have a lot of fun," Harry said.

We sat in the grandstands, among the great unwashed masses, noses stuck in programs, calculating, conniving, asking questions, looking for hot tips, snooping here and there, studying the tote board, and betting and winning and losing, laughing and cursing. Here, I thought, was the human race at its very best and its very worse, all at once. Here, I thought, were the parents of my junior high ninth grade English students.

I bought a round of hot dogs. Then Harry bought cokes. After the second race, Sheldon bought three big bags of popcorn. Harry and Sheldon had bet the Daily Double, a wagering strategy, I gathered, linking the winner of one race with the winner of another race. Harry put up a buck; Sheldon put up a buck. The last of the big time spenders. It's a good thing they didn't bet the farm because in the first race their choice beat a dog, and that's only because that dog fell down, and their choice in the second race might still be running out there somewhere. Last time I saw the dog it vanished into the shadows of the far turn. I don't know if it ever finished or not. So now Harry and Sheldon were behind, two dollars, and, gamblers that they were, they had their noses stuck in their programs, ferreting out the winner of the next race.

I had never been to a dog track before. Quite a spectacle, I had to admit, and entertaining. Eight dogs in colorful blankets came out onto the track, stood around for awhile in front of the grandstands, then moved on down to the starting boxes where they stood around some more. Then all the lights dimmed and a bell went off, and leadouts stuffed Greyhounds into starting boxes, and the mechanical rabbit started clattering around the track, and the announcer said *AND HEEEEEERE COMES WINDY.....*, then the bell quit, and the grandstand lights shut off, and the track lights came on and eight Greyhounds lunged from the starting boxes, and the announcer said *AND THERE THEY GO!!!!!!* and the dogs chased the fake rabbit, and in a moment it was over, and everybody carried on; some grew angry and booed and threw things; some became ecstatic and hugged and kissed everybody in sight. That all took place in thirty seconds and that's it..... winners in that line, losers remain seated and try again. Everybody ante up for the next one.

For some reason, the betting did not interest me. Maybe it was my Scotch heritage. I was too cheap to take a chance. But the dogs interested me. I could not believe anything could move so fast with such power, such grace, such determination.

I asked: "Where do they go?"

"What do you mean?" Harry said, circling the Number

16

Five dog in his program.

"I mean, where do they put the dogs when they're through racing."

"The trainers pick them up at the jinny pit, down there, then cool them off, out there." Harry pointed. "Just the other side of that fence."

"I'd like to see the dogs, up close. Do you think that'd be possible?"

"Sure. Don't see why not."

"This betting doesn't do it for me," I said. "I'm going to nose around a little. I'll be back in a race or two. If I can't get back in, I'll wait for you at the truck."

Neither looked up from the racing programs.

It was out in the dark, out behind the grandstands and the racing oval, out in the cool of the Montana night, where I first made contact with racing Greyhounds. I stood around, made small talk with the trainers, asked about this dog, or petted that dog. I met the likes of Mangy Martinez and Pooch the Mooch McGill. And Hugh and Elsie Mungas. And Ben Dover and Jake the Rake Smith and Dogbreath Smith, and Fleas Finnegan. They fascinated me, the way they talked, the way they worked with the dogs. I watched the dog people scrub the racers' paws, clean the nails, rub the legs with smelly liniments. It reminded me of what I had read of Hermes, and the way the Greeks used to take care of feet, first and foremost; I cautioned myself that Hermes was also the god of bums and thieves. Somebody said curiosity killed the cat. I had to meander along after the trainers and their dogs; I had to wander in to the kennel compounds, past the sign at the gate:

17

SECURITY AREA
AUTHORIZED PERSONNEL ONLY

You'd think an English teacher could read. Because I paid no attention to the sign, the path of my life was about to take a sharp, cattywampus detour.

I first saw him bent over, up against a kennel wall, grubbing around in a garbage can. The view of his enormous behind, was, well, what can I say, enormous.

"Lose something?" I asked.

"I think I threw out tomorrow's starters," he said, "and I can't for the life of me find them." He stood up to see who had spoken. For a moment I thought that he recognized me, but why in the world would he? He went back to grubbing in the garbage can.

"Take my program," I said. "Aren't these tomorrow's entries?" And I opened the program to the appropriate page.

He took a look.

"Yes. Thanks. Maddog McDermutt's the name," he said. "Greyhound's my game." He put out his hand.

"McNulty," I said. "Ryan McNulty. I'm a school teacher." And we shook hands.

Mr. McDermutt had on a rather strange uniform, I thought. It looked like a pink jump suit, something like a faded Santa suit, yellow mustard spilled down the front, a VOTE RE-PUBLICAN button on his chest, dirty cowboy hat, granny glasses, love beads, and a pair of boots unlike any other I had ever seen, something like Siberian cross-country ski boots, without skis. The boots were big, like size twenties, but I knew that was impossible. They just looked that big: clown feet, and they made him look deficient.

"McNulty, eh?" Mr. McDermutt muttered.

18

"Yes. I'm Scotch. My father was Scotch."

"Glasgow?"

"Oakland," I said.

And then he threw me a little Robert Burns.

Aw would the giftie give us
The gift to see ourselves as others see us.

I thought that was a rather strange verse to come up with. I was not sure if he wasn't a bum looking in the garbage can for dinner, or......... I was not sure. The ors were not coming easily.

"The best laid plans of mice and men often go awry." I said. I wanted Mr. McDermutt to realize he wasn't going to snow me that easily. I was, after all, an English teacher.

Mr. McDermutt promptly edited my quote. "The best laid plans of dogs and men often go flat bonkers," he said. "Furthermore, life is nothing more than a dog race. Somebody wins. Somebody loses. Who knows why. Are you interested in the Greyhounds?"

"Yes I am," I said. "Very much."

"Well, you came to the right place. You got lucky. I'll say that. Come here now, Ryan McNulty, and I'll show you the right thing."

He opened kennel door number nine, and I walked in. The room was full of crates. The crates were full of dogs. Racing Greyhounds. They stood up on our entrance.

Mr. McDermutt was immediately into a great bowl of what looked like slop to me, both hands, kneading it, throwing it, tossing it, pressing it, mashing it.

"It's my own recipe," he said. "Mostly horse meat, but a few other items in there that will make a hound get up and go."

"Can I help?"

And he started serving up the slop in dog bowls. "Start over there, that's right, open the gate, put the food in, close the gate, then come here, that's good, and the next one, no not the bottom, the top, that's it, now come on back, that's it."

And around the kennel I went. There must have been forty dogs in there.

When we were done, I watched Mr. McDermutt wash his hands. He looked me over carefully. "I want to show you something," he said.

He went to the end, on the bottom, and opened a door. Out stepped a gray brindle Greyhound, licking his chops from his recently gulped dinner. He was skinny as a rail. He was tall. This was a big Greyhound.

"Jones," Mr. McDermutt said.

"Jones?"

"Jones is from Australia. His racing name is Down Under Jones."

Mr. McDermutt paused to let that sink in.

"Australia's a long way home," I said.

"Tomorrow I have to put him to sleep," he said.

"What do you mean?" I asked.

"You know. The green needle. Bye Bye. Go to doggie heaven. Poor laddie buck graded off, and the owner doesn't want to go to the expense of feeding him anymore."

"What!"

I looked at the dog.

He came over, and I squatted. The dog put his cold nose

20

on my cheek and sniffed. I scratched his ear. He groaned. I ran my hand down his back. He sidled in to me, then sat down and leaned in to me. I petted him.

"Isn't he just the nicest fella you'd ever want to meet?" Mr. McDermutt said.

"He is a nice dog," I said, scratching the big dog's ears. I had the feeling I should not be out here.

what you need, McNulty, is a dog

"Of course I could always sell him to research for fifty bucks, but I won't do that. None of us here will do that. It's better to put the dog to sleep."

"Research?"

"Military. Vets. Sometimes they break their legs and see how they take to artificial joints. Usually they just kill them and vet students cut them up for practice."

I looked the big dog in the face. He gave me a big wet kiss, then stood there wagging his tail as I wiped my face with my sleeve.

"He's too big," Mr. McDermutt said. "He can't make the first turn. Other dogs cut the rail. Ol' Jones there, he works up a head of steam and just keeps going. By the time he makes it around the first turn, the rest are long gone."

"How old is he?"

"Oh, about a year and a half."

"How much do these dogs cost?" I asked.

"I think the owner paid three thousand for the litter. I don't know. Doesn't matter. Dog isn't for sale anyway."

"Why are his eyes so bloodshot?" I asked.

"He has something of a kidney problem," Mr. McDermutt said. "It's a chronic thing. These kennel compounds are bad for a dog like that. It's a chain-reaction thing. Kidneys demand water. Dog drinks. Signals get crossed. Kidneys can't handle the overload and demand more water. Crazy thing. He needs a place where he isn't kenneled like this, and the problem will go away, or my name is not Maddog McDermutt."

I gave the big dog a hug. He licked my ear. I was in over my head. My guts were churning. My head was spinning. Right then and there I became the dog's champion. I had the feeling Mr. McDermutt could read my mind.

"I said I couldn't sell him," Mr. McDermutt said.

"I heard you," I said.

"I might, however, be in a position to give 'im to ye," he said.

He let that sink in. I could tell this Mr. McDermutt was something of a judge of human nature. He knew very well he had a sap on the line.

what you need, McNulty, is a dog

"I have a rope," he said. "I'll give you the collar. You give big Jones there a good home, and I'd be grateful. You see, I like big Jones too. He's a good old boy, and he would make somebody a wonderful companion and ask little in return. There is little enough friendship in this world as it is. Looks like you need a friend. He needs a friend. And....I'll tell you something else; you treat a dog good, and the dog will return the favor. You don't sell your friends. This evening is a good luck charm. You, the dog, and me. When you take big Jones there, our destinies, you, the dog, and me, we three are intertwined forever."

I was not old enough to take a great deal of stock in bush-league mysticism. This wide-bottomed, pot-bellied, granny-glasses, pink jump suit, love beads, tarnished VOTE REPUB-LICAN button, yellow mustard-down-his-front Mr. McDermutt and I would be fatally intertwined forever? That was enough to run screaming from the kennel. But the allure of the big Greyhound at my side was strong.

Mr. McDermutt smiled. He opened the kennel door for me. "Take him for a run, once in awhile. Go chase a rabbit. Jones would highly enjoy that." Mr. McDermutt bent over and petted the big dog. Then he knelt down and gave the dog a big hug. "Take care, big fellow," he said to the dog.

And Jones licked his hand.

"That's a good dog," Mr. McDermutt said, giving the big Greyhound a final pat on the head.

"Come on, Jones," I said. We were out the kennel door.

what you need, McNulty, is a dog.

I opened the door to the cab of Harry's pickup. Jones jumped in like he had been jumping in pickup trucks all his life. I did not need to ask twice. I patted him on the neck. He was a big dog. He sat higher than I did. I straightened my back and stretched my neck and still his head was higher than mine. I looked him in the eye. "Well Jones, what do you think?"

He thumped his tail on the seat and slobbered on my coat sleeve.

More to the point. What would my wife think?

Harry appeared at the driver's door, Sheldon at the passenger door. They both stared in at Jones and me.

Finally, Harry said, "What's that?"

I said, "You said I should have a dog."

"That's not a dog. That's a Greyhound."

"What do you mean not a dog? A Greyhound's a dog. This is Jones. Down Under Jones meet Harry and Sheldon."

They climbed in, a little crowded, the four of us. As we pulled up to the Tenth Avenue stoplight, Jones gave Harry a big wet kiss, which Sheldon found humorous.

"What are you going to do with this monstrosity?" Harry asked, wiping his face with his sleeve.

"You said I ought to have a dog. You said every teacher ought to have a dog."

"That's true," Sheldon said. "We certainly did."

At this particular point in time, Jones, and I presume it was Jones, and I would most certainly like to point out it was not I, did a bad thing. Sheldon and Harry rolled down their windows.

"Cripes," Harry said, eyeball to eyeball with Jones. "What on this round earth have they been feeding you?"

Jones started to pant.

"Something dead a very long time," Sheldon said. He stuck his head out the window.

"It's Mr. McDermutt's special mix," I said. "It's his own formula, a secret."

"Thank heavens," Harry said.

Harry pulled up in front of my house. Sheldon got out. I slid over and out, pushing Jones ahead of me.

"Thanks for a great time," I said. "See you tomorrow Third Period."

Harry looked the dog and me over, put his truck into gear, and drove off.

I walked my new dog up the sidewalk. I opened the door

and stepped in. Jones stepped in. My wife came around the corner, stopped, and stared. I looked down at the dog. His bloodshot eyes, glistening in the living room lamp light, did create something of a demon from Hell.

"Has a kidney problem," I said.

We stood there a moment more. I was sure we were about to be asked to leave.

"His name is Jones," I said. "Down Under Jones. He's from Australia. Jones, this is Sally." I scratched him on the ears. He looked at Sally, whined, and wagged his tail. "They were going to ..... " I felt a tear run down my cheek.

Sally sat down in the easy chair and looked at the big Greyhound. "Hello Jones," she said.

And the dog walked over to say hello, his tail going back and forth, and Sally petted the dog, and that night Jones moved right in, slept at the foot of the bed, and I dreamed of an old Scot dog trainer in a pink jump suit, a VOTE REPUBLICAN button on his chest, love beads around his neck, yellow mustard stains down his front, Siberian cross-country ski boots making him look like he would never tip over. He was driving a pickup truck pulling a dog trailer, and he was driving into the night, away from Great Falls, Montana, driving far, far away, and tomorrow I would go teach English to ninth graders at Paris Gibson Junior High, and somehow, somehow I knew that I would cross paths with Mr. Maddog McDermutt again. I had no idea how, or why, or when. But it would be so.

The dog sleeping at the foot of the bed.

McDermutt.

And me.

THREE

The alarm went off. Monday.

"School days," Sally said. "Good old golden rule days."

"I don't think I slept very much last night," I said. "What is wrong with my leg?"

"It has a big dog wrapped around it."

I looked. Sure enough. "Jones doesn't seem to know it is Monday," I said.

"Do you suppose in the future Jones can find another place to sleep?" Sally suggested.

I looked the dog over.

One eyelid cranked open, blinked at Sally.

"Let's not discuss it in front of him," I said.

Sally had hold of the bedspread. "This is damp," she said. Then, with much more feeling, and with a finger pointed right at the dog, she said, "That dog wet the bed!"

Jones's head shot up. He looked around, like who is she talking to? The dog stared at me, bloodshot eyes, cocked ears, a couldn't-be-me look on his face. He stared at me, cut loose with a door-slamming burst of gas.

"Wow!" I said.

"Good heavens!" Sally gasped.

"Those kidneys could be a problem," I said, reaching down to scratch his ear.

Jones lifted his head, moaned and turned his head so that I could scratch it correctly. Harry and Sheldon had been right. Ever since I had started teaching I had never been so relaxed on a Monday morning. "How about if I take him to the vet, after school, you know, check it out. Maybe there's something they can give him: pills, a shot, something."

"Fine. But for now you'd better motivate yourself on down to school. First year teachers don't want to be late."

First Period, and I was well into Chapter Five of good old Sir Walter Scott's IVANHOE, when an office aid, a freckle-faced girl in the vicinity of fourteen, with flaming red-hair and an Attila the Hun haircut, a purple ribbon holding all that up, and a short, short purple skirt, skinny legs, and heavily painted lips, and heavily painted eyebrows, one eyebrow raised with great sophistication, that eye therein that socket eyeing me curiously, something like the eye of a fish, handed over a note like she was casting for the new junior high sleaze role in the spring melodrama production. The note was open, and so I knew the office aid had read it, provided, of course, she could read in the first place. The aid, watching me closely, blew a great pink bubble.

JONES RAN OFF. YOUR WIFE.

I read over the note a couple of times, wondering what I was supposed to do, then set it on the desk, then said to the office aid: "Would you mind? That gum is disgusting."

The bubble broke. The pink stuff covered her mouth and her chin and her cheeks, almost ear to ear, and almost covered her eyes, but it did not faze her. She sucked and snorted and sucked and smacked and sucked, the tongue here, there, and the gum withdrew past her overdone lips and into her empty head. I found the whole thing revolting. I would have to mention this later to somebody up in the office. My nerve endings were warming up. Not too many things around school bothered me. Gum was one of them. I hadn't been teaching a quarter yet, and I had come to hate the stuff.

Rubber lips turned and tried to walk (I'm sure she thought of it as sexy) down the aisle. The problem was that there wasn't any fanny there to wriggle, and so the effect, from my point of view, was something like a field scarecrow moving down two rows of corn. One of my female ninth graders, curious to a fault, leaned over and in a frog-throated stage whisper, said, "What'd the note say?"

And the aid said, in an equally loud stage whisper, for all to hear, poking her thumb over her shoulder at me, the trashy individual at the teacher's desk, "Some guy ran off with his wife."

And the class gasped.

"Geeez," I said, shaking my head at the departing aid.

"Guy's name is Jones," she said, turning to blow a big bubble. She leaned against the door frame, one leg stuck out, her chest with nothing to brag about all puffed out. She looked over her bright red nails and fluttered her fake eyelids as she said: "Jones." The bubble banged shut across her face on her exit. "The name is Jones."

I held up the note to the class and pointed to it. "It says," I said, reading it for them, "**JONES RAN OFF. YOUR WIFE**. It does not say **JONES RAN OFF WITH YOUR WIFE**."

I looked at the class look at me.

"Back to <u>IVANHOE</u>" I said. "Lucy, why don't you read from where we left off. Thank you very much."

And Lucy read <u>IVANHOE</u> with meaningful depth, I thought. And then Fred read, then Mary, then Jack, and down the second row, and the bell rang and I said, "Finish the chapter for tomorrow," and I ran upstairs to the phone and called home.

"Golly, Sally. What happened?"

"I let Jones out the back door, and he sniffed around, lifted his leg on the garbage can, looked both ways in the alley, then wandered out of sight behind the garage. I rushed right after him, and he had vanished. I'm so sorry."

"It isn't your fault."

"I called *HERE JONES*!!!! over and over until I have a sore throat," Sally said. "I've called all the neighbors we know to be on the lookout. I've been all around the area; I've been around several blocks, door to door."

"I should never have accepted responsibility for that dog," I said. "I am the general all-around fool of the year. That Mr. McDermutt pulled a good one. Pawned a worthless dog off on me that won't come when it's called and P's its bed. He P's my bed. I'll bet McDermutt is chuckling about his little coup all the way to Florida."

I thought about it, then said: "Well, I suppose we are legally liable in that I accepted the dog. Call the office and leave a message if Jones shows up. I have to be in Second Period."

And so it went, the periods dragging by, and finally the school day was over, and I went home a fretting wreck. By now I think I had covered all the possibilities:

The dog was totally lost. A Greyhound is a sight hound, not a nose hound. He hadn't been at our address long enough to remember anything. And that is taking in to consideration he had a brain in the first place, to remember anything with. Awful possibilities took a turn running by my brain: the dog would be run over by a car; the dog would be killed by a car; the dog would be maimed by a car; the car would be maimed by the dog; the pound would pick him up and he would catch some terrible disease; he would bite somebody; he would kill somebody's little dog or cat; he would find himself in a dog fight and lose; he would find himself in a dog fight and win, and I would find myself in a lawsuit; he would lose his head and run himself to death; somebody who didn't care about dogs would find him and mistreat him; he would starve; he would bite a biker; attack a jogger; nail the mailman, a federal offense. The possibilities were endless. Maddog McDermutt said the dog had a kidney problem. For all I knew those bloodshot eyes were the first signs of distemper, or the plague, or the Apocalypse.

That afternoon we drove all over our neighborhood. We drove one block in every direction, looking into driveways, open-door garages, then drove two blocks, stepped out, knocked on doors. "Have you seen a large, skinny gray brindle Greyhound today?"

Nobody had seen Jones.

"The dog is probably in somebody's house, taking a nap on the living room rug," I said. But neither of us believed it.

That night I went to bed and tried to sleep, but didn't. I heard barking dogs all night. One to the south; one to the north; several dogs to the east. I had not learned Jones's bark. Were any of the barks that of a Greyhound? It was a long night.

The next day at school I fretted through each class, then when the bell rang I rushed upstairs to the office to phone home. Each time nothing. I told each period about my missing dog, and once they had it in their heads Jones was a dog, particularly Period One, I told them about the race track adoption. The kids promised to keep all eyes open, and they had friends and relatives around town they could ask too. The principal did not seem to understand the situation upon my explanation, and I have to admit I was not surprised, but the vice principal of the school was kind enough to broadcast an announcement to the student body over the loud speaker, that I had lost my dog, a tall Greyhound, and to be on the lookout, and give me a call at my home if anybody saw him or even heard something. We had about 1,000 kids in school, plus teachers, plus support personnel. A good start, I thought.

Third period prep period, Harry and Sheldon looked me over pretty good. Harry thought that the dog wandering off was a blessing, give it a week or two, then go buy a real dog. Sheldon said the pound probably picked him up, and I'd have to bail him out plus pay for shots plus pay a fine for his running loose. I might even have to go to court to answer a nuisance charge. Neither Harry nor Sheldon upped my spirits much.

At 4:30 the phone rang.

A parent wanted to know what the assignment for her absent Billy was.

"Chapter Seven, <u>IVANHOE</u>," I said.

She closed by saying she hoped we found our lost dog.

"Thanks," I said.

Dinner. No more calls.

I read compositions until 11:30.

No calls.

If by tomorrow after school I had not heard anything, I would step up the search. I wanted to know where my dog was. I hoped those dogs wouldn't bark all night, off in the distance like that. I wondered if they had seen Jones. Maybe one of them was barking at Jones. I thought about checking that out, but I was too tired. Too tired to think; too tired to sleep. I lay there, in a daze, depressed.

Wednesday more of the same: no word. Nothing. I called the pound. Nothing. I called the fire department, the cab company, the bus company, and the police department. I figured they covered the town fairly well, sooner or later. Nothing. Then I called THE TRIBUNE, and a writer said because the track had closed for good, and I didn't know that, that he would run a little story on the giveaway Greyhound. Jones was going to get some ink. Both television stations said they would throw it into their news programs, as long as the paper was doing something. Once I found out the media thought like that, I then called all the radio stations while I was at it. They were lukewarm enthusiastic, but if the paper and TV stations were interested, why not. By now the theme had become a constant.

RACING GREYHOUND ON THE LOOSE

A 75 pound male Greyhound, gray brindle, tall, lanky, bloodshot eyes, has vanished. Anyone seeing this lost animal should call English teacher Ryan McNulty at 555-2108.

That was Wednesday night on both the two television stations.

Thursday morning the GREAT FALLS TRIBUNE hit the streets with this story:

> Paris Gibson Junior High School English teacher Ryan McNulty offered to give a home to a retiring racing Greyhound on the close of the Great Falls Dog Track.The dog has vanished. Nobody has seen this dog in the last three days. The dog is male, tall, gray brindle, eighteen months old. Mr. McNulty is offering a small reward for the return of his dog.

"Where'd they get that?" I muttered, tossing the newspaper. I did not offer a reward for that miserable dog. Yes, I was worried about him. Yes, I wanted him back. No, I did not say he was worth a plugged nickel. All I did was save him from death, or research.

4:30 PM Thursday: a call came in.

Somebody had seen Jones!

"Hey Sally!" I called. "Somebody has seen the dog."

She put her ear to the phone and we both listened.

"Yes, this is the party with the missing Greyhound," I said.

"This is Captain Weatherall out at Base Security."

Malmstrom Air Force Base? Malmstrom was five miles to the east. You couldn't go further east and still be in Great Falls, Montana.

"Your dog went through our security check-point Charlie at 10:30 Tuesday morning. The airman on duty called the dog, but the dog seemed deaf. The dog had purpose, you know, like he knew where he was going. The dog urinated on the fire hydrant on the corner of the Base Command Control Center Building. Then he headed for the airfield, via the Officer's Club, the Enlisted Men's Club, and a trailered Minuteman Missile, and by this time we had a security car and two Air Force Police on his tail, because that is a very high security area, and that dog ran around the PX so fast we almost lost him right there, but the dog found himself on the airfield itself, paused to lift his leg on a transport plane's tire. Then he went across the strip right by our fighter jets. Then he headed south. He treated the corner fence post, then he headed west, back toward 10th Avenue South, and he went under a barbed wire fence, and our security car could not follow, and that is the last we saw of him."

"And that was Tuesday?"

"Yes Sir. That's a Roger."

"Thank you very much," I said. "Did the dog look all right?"

"Yes Sir. Moving right along, just fine."

"Well thank you, Captain. We certainly do appreciate the call."

I hung up the phone.

The phone rang again.

And again.

And again.

And again.

The phone never quit ringing until twelve-thirty.

Jones had been seen. Everybody in Great Falls had seen Jones.

The most encouraging call came in from the trout hatchery, except that the event preceded, chronologically, the Malmstrom Air Force Captain's call. Monday morning Jones had stopped to drink at a Giant Springs trout hatchery runway. The Montana Fish and Game employee said a gray brindle Greyhound took five minutes to drink from the runway. The dog acted like he was dehydrated. Then, finished with that, he wandered to the Missouri River to drink another five minutes. Then he drank more from Giant Springs itself. The man said he didn't know why the dog didn't blow up. Then he mentioned the dog relieved himself on the corner of the concession stand, on the trout hatchery guest registry, and squirted every car tire on his way out the parking lot, heading due east.

"Well," I said to Sally, at the end of the evening. "It sounds like Jones is running a pattern. I think tomorrow we can head him off over in the Mountain View area."

"Maybe," Sally said. "Do you think he really knows where he is going?"

I wanted to say he did. "No," I said. "He's a dog. He has no map. He can't read street signs. He has wandered down to Giant Springs, then he wandered out to Malmstrom. Combined, that must be eight miles, maybe nine, maybe ten. He's lost, no doubt about it. The dog has spent his life on a Greyhound farm or in a kennel at a dog track. All of a sudden he is lost in a city."

I sat up in bed and shouted: "The dog track! How could I be so stupid. Why didn't I think of that before? Jones is looking for the dog track. This isn't home, the dog track is."

"What?"

"The dog track. Jones is looking for the dog track. It is the only thing that makes sense."

"The only thing that makes sense is that you are missing your sleep and you are going to make yourself sick."

"The dog track," I said. "I have to go to the dog track. You stay here. I'll drive out and take a quick look. I'll never get to sleep if I don't." I was stepping into my pants. "I'll be right back." I had my shoes on. "I won't be long," I said, and I was out the door, on the way.

I drove around the dog track parking lot, over to the kennel compounds, and right on to the track itself; the gate had been left open, like nobody cared any more. I stuck my head out the window and called. And called. And called. My voice echoed around the empty grandstands. Then I walked the property, fence to fence, past where the tote was, around the kennels, opened the door of Maddog McDermutt's kennel and looked in. Nothing. Then I drove down Tenth Avenue South and ordered a hamburger at a fast food establishment; then I ordered another in case I found my dog, he'd be hungry, then I returned to the track and called and called and called.

I left the hamburger on the rail at the finish line, drove for home, went to bed.

The next day, Thursday, we had a phone call from a lady who had seen Jones crossing Gibson Flats, an undeveloped area south of Great Falls.

"Golly," I said to Sally on my way out the door, "that's five miles behind the track. What's this dog running on?"

Thursday afternoon we drove all over the south side of

town, from Giant Springs to Malmstrom, from Malmstrom to Gibson Flats, from Gibson Flats to Fox Farm Road, and up and down the Missouri River on both sides. Occasionally we would stop to ask a taxi driver, a cop, a pedestrian, a couple of kids on bikes, a lady watering her lawn, "Have you seen a gray tall skinny Greyhound?"

I expected strange looks, like sure buddy, right after the pink elephant, but characteristically it was....Oh yeah sure. I saw that dog yesterday, right over there........yes, I saw that dog heading across the park........I saw that dog drinking out of my lawn sprinkler.......I saw that dog sprinkling tires in the Holiday Village shopping mall parking lot......He was right over there...lifting his leg on my favorite rose bush."

Enough. I pulled out a set of compositions. I was more behind in my work than ever.

"It's Fard Worthington," my wife said, handing over the phone.

"Who?" I asked, setting my papers down.

"Fard Worthington."

What kind of a name was that?

I spoke into the phone. "Hello?"

A young, scratchy voice said, "Mr. McNulty, have you found your dog yet?"

"No, I haven't. Who are you?"

"Fard Worthington, Mr. McNulty. Fardington Maddog Worthington. I am Maddog McDermutt's godson. I live in Ulm."

"Fardington Maddog Worthington?"

My wife's eyebrows raised. I nodded.

"Yes Mr. McNulty. Maddog's only godson. You can call

me Fard. Maddog does. Our family is into Greyhound racing also. We own the famous derby dog brood bitch Miss Neopolitan, and my father owned the greatest Greyhound the world has ever known, the unforgettable Mr. Inspiration, trained by none other than my godfather Maddog McDermutt. I read about your missing dog and phoned my godfather, who is now racing in Key West, Florida. Ironically, Mr. McNulty, I did not know that my godfather Maddog himself had given you the Greyhound. Small world, eh? Godfather McDermutt said your dog is checking out his territory. When a dog moves in to new territory, his first and foremost obligation, to himself and to his neighbors, is to stake it out, to squirt all four corners and selected points. This is where I live, the squirt says, and, squirt, squirt, squirt, trespassers cross that line at their own perils."

"Well, we've had reports of him all over town," I said.

A lull, then I said, "The dog is lost."

"Great Falls is a fairly good-sized town," Fard said. "If I had taken that Greyhound, he would have staked out this little town of Ulm in not more than a day or two. It'll take your dog maybe a week to cover Great Falls. Additionally, my godfather, Maddog McDermutt, says that your dog is taking his chronic kidney problem into his own hands. Your dog is going to keep going until his kidneys kick in with the right signals. He is doctoring himself, so to speak. He is going to kill it or cure it."

"Right," I said. I was really beginning to feel the weariness of the last few days in my bones. I ached all over. "Now you're going to tell me that old dog trainer Maddog McDermutt is a doctor. I don't want to discredit your godfather, young man, but I doubt he has a degree in medicine. And that Greyhound certainly does not have a degree in veterinary science."

"I was just trying to be helpful. Good-bye, Mr. McNulty." And he hung up.

"Strange young man," I commented to Sally. "He thinks Jones is staking out his territory. "He's saying, *I live here. This is my territory. You cross that line at your own peril.*"

Friday came and went. The calls stopped. The dog had vanished.

Saturday I slept in, then arose to read the paper, nothing of interest there; then I ripped a map of the city of Great Falls out of the phone book and pinned it to the wall. We identified all the phone call points with pins. Giant Springs to Malmstrom to Gibson Flats. "Well," I said. "If he is circling the city, and I have to admit it sort of looks like it, next stop Gore Hill and the Great Falls International Airport."

On the seventh day we had calls that Jones had been seen over in Black Eagle, clean across town. So much for Fard Worthington's circle theory. "The dog is a goner," I said. "He'll never survive the bridge at rush hour."

"Can a Greyhound swim?" Sally asked.

Sunday: No Jones. No more phone calls. We waited up until 10:30. If I was going to make any sense at all in school tomorrow, I had to place my tired body to bed and give it some sleep. I did, and morning I was up to check the front door, and the back door, but still no Jones.

The dog had to be starving.

In the middle of First Period, the same old messenger, same old look on her face, brought in a note from the office.

The note said:

LOOK OUT YOUR WINDOW

I looked out the classroom window. Standing on the sidewalk was a very skinny gray brindle Greyhound. "Jones!" I said, trying to open the window. The window was jammed. Again. Should I run out of the room and try to coax him to me? I watched the dog lift his leg on a student's lunch box, left on the sidewalk, and give a small, quick squirt. The dog looked tired. Tired? He looked shot. He looked like he had crawled out of hell itself. It looked like he had recently walked around Great Falls, Montana. And here he was, a week later, on the sidewalk of Paris Gibson Junior High, squirting some kid's lunch box.

One student said, "Isn't that your dog, Mr. McNulty?"

I nodded. "Yup. What's left of him."

"Hey, it's Down Under Jones!" And all the kids ran to the window.

"All right!" one said.

"I thought he was lost."

"He was," I said.

"Hey! That's my lunch box!" Fred said.

"Man, that is a big Greyhound. Look at that sucker, I'll bet he stands on his hind legs he's taller than you," and Joe pointed to the tallest kid in the class who was a modest six feet. The kids started tapping on the windows.

"Don't," I said. "You'll frighten him."

Jones looked up at the window. It was uncanny. He was looking right at me. He knew me? He knew where I was? The big dog wagged his tail. His eyes were clear! He stepped up to the bronze plaque PARIS GIBSON JUNIOR HIGH

SCHOOL and gave it a fine squirt; any dog would have been proud. The class cheered. And then Jones was on the move, trotting, moving east, and I watched him pause at Fifteenth, to let the traffic pass, and when the light changed, he crossed the street, still heading east on Second Avenue, and I knew that he knew where he was going. This dog would not get run over by a car. This dog was not lost. This dog knew exactly what he was doing. In about three minutes he would be sniffing and scratching at our back door, and Sally would let him in and feed him. He had no maps; he could not read street signs; this Australian transplant with the name of Down Under Jones had been gone one full week from a house in the middle of Great Falls, population 75,000, a house he had known only for one night, and now he was zeroing in on that house, and the military couldn't have done a better job with all of its sophisticated tracking equipment.

"There goes some kind of dog," I muttered.

As the class reseated itself, I thought for a moment I saw a reflection in the window, of a man in a pink jump suit, with granny glasses and love beads, saying, *you, me, and the dog.* I looked at the class. The class was looking at me, grinning, happy for me my dog was back.

"We're all glad your dog is OK," a spokesman said.

"Do you think some day we could see him run?" Mary, in the back of the room, asked.

"Sure," I said. "That would be fun."

And here came the office aid again. She swaggered up to my desk, put a note on the desk, with one painted nail holding it down with authority, like, OK, let's see how you handle this one, dirt bag.

I read the note.

JONES HOME. EXHAUSTED.

I brushed the tear away, and smiled, and tried to explain to this muttonhead: "My dog came home."

She grunted, blew a big bubble, snapped it, and headed down the aisle. She paused to jerk her thumb at me, then said, "This guy has big problems."

Over the school PA came the announcement:

WE ARE HAPPY TO REPORT
THAT MR. MCNULTY'S DOG JONES
HAS RETURNED.

The class cheered and applauded.

In the middle of Sixth Period, the same dippy office aid was standing at my desk with yet another note, this time a Western Union telegram, and I was wondering if all she did all day long was deliver notes; she probably took office aid six periods a day to avoid anything academic. She was tapping her finger impatiently on the desk as I read it, dated September 10, 1:30 P.M., Key West, Florida

TOLD YOU SO. MADDOG

"And you young lady," I said, killing two birds with one stone, "you may spit that awful pink bubble gum, right here," and I held out the telegram, and she, with great indignity, plucked the gum from her now empty head, and placed the gum in the telegram which I crumpled in my fist.

And in the can went telegram and gum. "You, You, and You," I said to the can, note, and gum, "are intertwined forever. And good-bye."

FOUR

It didn't take me long to look forward to afternoons, to take my dog for a walk after school. Harry and Sheldon had been right. Jones was what the doctor ordered. Jones always met me at the door, tail wagging, head out for a pat. While I changed out of my school duds into my walk-around-the-plains Levis, boots, jacket, hat, sun glasses, Jones would sit by the door and wait, his tail thumping the floor.

Every afternoon we drove out of town, out into the middle of nowhere, out onto the vast Montana prairies and wheatlands, to see if we couldn't find a Montana jack rabbit to course.

We varied our sojourns from day to day. One day we headed south; then north; today we walked east out behind the air base; rolling country, rows of winter wheat, rows of stubble, rows of fallow, punctuated by Missouri River coulees, fingers of rough, unworked hard native ground, with rocks, bush grass, cactus, snakes, and tough little bushes, tough and wild enough to defy man's encroachment of the plow. At night the rabbits came out of the coulees to graze in the stubble fields, and if the weather was right, when daybreak came, they didn't return; they sunned behind clumps of dirt in the plowed parts, and once in awhile we would come across one. We could, if we felt like it, go all the way down a coulee to the Missouri, cut over the rise, and come back up another coulee, all in all a walk of several miles.

I stopped the truck, stepped out, opened the door, and out jumped Jones. He walked around the truck, then lifted his leg and gave the front left tire a good squirt, staring, casually, out across the prairie. He continued to stand there, his leg frozen in the salute position. I looked out across the prairie too.

I didn't have to look far. Standing not more than ten yards away, staring back at us, was an exceptionally large Montana hare.

Big ears, brown this time of year, not white; maybe as much as ten pounds. Maybe more. This guy was bigger than a big house cat. He seemed to have little fear of us; he watched us curiously. I could not help but notice a distinctive mark over his left shoulder, a scar maybe, a birthmark, but a very definite flag on the left shoulder.

Jones continued to stare. I thought maybe he might put his leg down by now, but the big dog remained frozen there.

Jones glanced at me, like is what I'm looking at really what I'm looking at?

The rabbit moved away, slowly, like hoping we might not notice.

"Mate," I said in my best Australian drawl, "will you be remaining in that position, or will it be a bit of a chase?"

The dog looked at me and barked.

"No prizes for barking," I said. The rabbit started a slow hop, hop, hop; Jones dropped his leg to the ground and took several steps forward, on his tippy-toes; the rabbit stopped; the dog stopped; the rabbit jumped, then bounced, ker plop, ker plop, ker plop, and Jones was trotting, looking over his shoulder to see if I thought it was all right, and I said, "Hey man, don't rush into anything," then Jones took a run at the rabbit; the rabbit performed a little sidestep; Jones went buns over teakettles on the passby, shoulder, back, rear end, a bouncing dog. The rabbit quit fooling around, found a new gear, hunkered down low to the ground, and he was out of there, over the rise and gone. Jones never had a chance. Unsighted, the dog came back to walk at my side, ribs heaving, tongue hanging out.

"I can see why you were asked to leave the track," I said. I scratched his ears. "So who cares."

Only a week ago I had phoned Fardington Worthington in Ulm for Maddog McDermutt's address so that I could write and tell him Jones and I were running Montana jacks on a regular basis. Fard said that Maddog McDermutt said that the Montana jack is faster than an antelope and can do right angles at fifty miles an hour. Although I suspected Maddog might stretch the truth some, I said to Jones: "Those Montana jacks are impossible."

The dog wagged his tail.

We rounded out the afternoon by walking all the way down a coulee to the Missouri River and returned to the truck via the next coulee. We saw no more rabbits. Jones jumped up onto the seat of the truck, tongue hanging out, panting, plopping down, ready to call it a day.

The next day in First Period, a student asked: "How's your racing Greyhound, Mr. McNulty?"

So I told him, as the rest of the class listened in, about our walks. I said that yesterday I had taken my racing Greyhound Jones out behind Malmstrom Air Force Base for a walk, and

47

that Jones saw a jack rabbit, and how the event had gone. I had a foreign exchange student from Paris, France, in the class, and I spelled on the board J A C K R A B B I T, and he enthusiastically joined in, saying, "Eh.. Jacques Ra...beet." And everyone thought that humorous. Then Sandy had to ask why the jack rabbit was called a jack rabbit, and I said I had no idea, and so I sent Sandy to the library, and Sandy came back with at least ten different definitions, and none of them quite fit, and so I told the class I would find out for sure. I would call a real authority, and let them know tomorrow, and it was now time to do some grammar, at which time I was booed loudly.

That evening I phoned Maddog McDermutt who said:

"Why everybody knows that one. Jackass! Because of the ears and body shape. Jack Ass. Jack Rabbit."

I really did not like the way he said Jackass.

The next day I reported back to the kids, reminding them that it might be erroneous on account of the source. "In fact," I added, "the information might even be autobiographical."

The following Tuesday I parked the truck in exactly the same place. Jones jumped out. I loved to watch him move. He was gaining weight every day. His muscles bulged; his coat was shiny; his eyes were clear; he seemed to float as he moved.

Déjà vu!!!!!

In exactly the same place was exactly the same rabbit with exactly the same flag on the shoulder looking at us in exactly the same way.

This time Jones was not paralyzed at the tire and didn't hesitate. He was, as they say at the dog track, off and running. And so was Jacques Ra...beet. "Go Jacques!" I yelled, and he did. That rabbit could haul. Jones went buns-over-teakettles on the first dodge, then he was up again, and off they went across the prairie, this way, then that way, zigs, and zags, then Jacques ran up over the rise with a burst of easy speed, having exhausted the dog on quick turns, the last we saw of Jacques Ra...beet this day.

We took a stroll down the coulee to the river and back and went home.

The days went by. Every so often we drove out behind Malmstrom Air Force Base, and every time Jacques Ra...beet was behind his usual clump of dirt. It was as if the old jack was waiting for us. And every time Jones thought he had the whole thing down, old Jacques would add a new twist, a new cut, a different trajectory to his hole. Now at this time all jack rabbit aficionados start to scoff: jack rabbits ordinarily don't go down holes; they even "nest" above ground. Well I'm here to tell you that we chased Jacques down his hole so many times he had to be registered with the United States Postal Service; that was his address. Jacques would reach the hole about twenty yards ahead of Jones, wait a moment to check everything out, then down the hole he went, recreation finished for the day. Jones would hit the hole at about forty, throw on the brakes, the dust would fly, and he would sniff, and sniff, and sniff, and maybe dig a little, until I called, and he came, and we loaded up and went home. I started bringing Jacques carrots, and when the chase was over, I dropped them down the hole. I know he ate them, because they weren't there the next time.

Only once did the general thrust of our rendezvous with Jacques Ra...beet vary, over a period of a month. Fall was here, winter was around the corner, and Jacques was turning

49

white. But his habits didn't change. I personally think he looked forward to our presence and the run to his hole. But one time he nearly bit the bullet. One time, for some reason, Jones did not jump right out of the truck and head for the clump of dirt where all the fun was; he headed out past it, like maybe he had seen something, and then as long as he was out there, he headed for the hole, looked it over, then sat next to it. At this time, Jacques, who had been behind his clod of dirt all the time, popped up and started trotting across the prairie. The jack sized up Jones, already at his hole, then made a big circle, but Jones was going to be cute; he remained sitting by the hole. Jacques Ra...beet took a run straight at Jones, bouncing along, then turned a right angle, directly in front of Jones's nose. That did it. Jacques paid Jones back in spades. That day Jacques never did go down the hole; he led Jones a merry chase the big dog would never forget. Jacques let Jones catch up, gave the tiring dog hope, then whoosh!.... off he'd go in a big burst of speed. Finally, the jack rabbit tired of the day's activity and vanished over a rise. Jones collapsed on the prairie. He lay there, his eyes wide, gasping for air. I had to drive the truck to him. It took Jones three days to recover. It was on a Friday afternoon when we pulled up to the same spot, stopped the truck, let Jones out. Jones rushed over to the clump of dirt: nothing. No Jacques Ra....beet. We walked down to the river. There had been a fresh snow but no jack rabbit tracks. We came up the adjacent coulee, hit the road, and headed back for the car, when Jones ran over to the side of the road, sniffing something in the borrow pit. I moved on over there.

It was Jacques. He had been shot. A .22 hole identified itself behind his left ear.

The unmistakable mark on the shoulder left no doubt; I felt a terrible loss, and I think Jones did too. Why didn't Jacques jump up and run? Jones sniffed his carcass, and then, finally, bored, he moved off down the road toward the car. "Jacques," I said to the rabbit as a parting salute, "I'm sorry. Thanks for all the good runs. We are indebted."

Sometimes now and then, at home on the living room rug, Sally and I would catch Jones dreaming about Jacques Ra....beet, and the nose would twitch, and the legs would jerk; and from the throat came growls and whines; lying on his side, sound asleep, the dog was running full tilt out there on the Montana prairies. The dog would start panting; then suddenly his own bark would wake himself, and he would raise his head to look at me, and I would pat him on the head and scratch him behind an ear and tell him he was dreaming. I had to wonder. I remembered a clumsy buns-over-teakettles Greyhound, too tall and skinny for his own good, now a 102 pound running machine. I wondered what it would be like to take this dog back to the race track. I wondered what Maddog McDermutt might think of that idea. Thanks to our runs, and Jacques Ra....beet, I'd like to see the Greyhound that could take my Greyhound once around the oval.

you, me, and the dog

I tried to concentrate on my homework: <u>ROMEO AND JULIET: Act II</u>. I was having trouble keeping ahead of the kids on this one.

I put Shakespeare down, went in the other room, asked Sally: "Where'd I put McDermutt's phone number?"

FIVE

Sooner or later I knew that I would find my way out to Ulm to pay a visit to young Fard Worthington, Maddog McDermutt's godson. I guess it was inevitable I would want to see another Greyhound. Maybe I wanted Fard Worthington to see what my Greyhound looked like. I was not above bragging up my sleek and noble companion. I suffered Harry and Sheldon and their stories about their hunting dogs; even in prep period I once in awhile managed to sneak in a good word about my dog. Jones looked so good these days, as far as I was concerned, he could have come in from the planet Krypton: Super Dog! 102 pounds of solid muscle!

Jones sat on the passenger side of the pickup truck, taking in the passing Gore Hill, the airport terminals, the Air National Guard, the windmills that pumped water, and the wheat fields stretching to the Rockies beyond, punctuated here and there with a farmhouse, a barn and some big machinery parked nearby, a horse in a coral, Russian olives and cottonwood windbreaks, a vast, wide-open country, magnificent in its vastness. When I turned off the freeway at Ulm, Jones stood up at the stop sign, ready to jump out, but sat down again as the truck moved forward and through the town of Ulm. Jones and I watched the bar go by, the grocery store, the post office, the gas station; then he looked at me, like, that's it?

"Yep," I said, reaching over and scratching his ear. "That was Ulm, Montana." I slowed down to read the mailboxes of rural Ulm, Montana. I read them aloud and on each name Jones's ears perked, then relaxed.

"Adams. Nope."

"Yorlinski. Nope.

"Cranston. Nope.

"White. Nope."

"Worthington. Yup."

Jones stood up.

I turned down the lane and pulled to a stop in front of the gate to the house. As I stepped out of the truck and called Jones to do the same, I saw who I presumed to be Fard Worthington coming out the door to meet us, down the lane. Now here was Mr. Western, Mr. Montana, Mr. Cowboy. This guy was the one the rest of the moving picture characters called "Shorty." The boy, and he was short, was right out of a Hollywood western: Stetson cowboy hat, scarf around his neck, faded cotton shirt, probably used to be green, blue, or blue/green, Levis jacket, collar up, leather patches on the elbows, Levis pants, patches on the knees and butt, leather belt with a huge belt buckle, I'll say six inches wide by three inches tall, inscribed F.A.R.D., brown, leather work gloves, and high-heeled, pointy, unshined cowboy boots. To complete the metaphor, the boy walked bowlegged, like he spent sixteen hours a day on a horse. He clomped by and around the gate, around a mailbox inscribed WORTHINGTON which suddenly exploded with a noisy swarm of black flies, thousands of flies, a cloud so thick you couldn't see through it. As Fard passed the mailbox, the cloud seemed to recognize him, imploded and silenced. I blinked. I couldn't see or hear a fly anywhere. I expected Fard to drawl, "Hi y'all, how y'all doin'?"

Fard said, "Mr. McNulty, I presume."

"Yes."

Fard swept a glove from his right hand, and we shook hands.

"Wow," Fard said, working his fingers back into his glove. "That is some kind of Greyhound. What do you feed that monster?" Fard reached out and patted Jones on the back. "You have a saddle? I would like to go for a ride. Just kidding. My godfather Maddog McDermutt said the dog was the biggest racing Greyhound he had ever raced, but Mr. McNulty this dog is an absolute monster. What does he weigh?"

"102 pounds, naked."

"Very good, Mr. McNulty. A sense of humor helps when it comes to dogs. Well, now that I have seen your dog, perhaps you would like to see my dog, Miss Neopolitan."

"Sure would."

"Follow me, please," and Fard Worthington swaggered off, leading the way to the barn. He shoved open a door, and we entered. Fard looked in the horse stalls; he looked in all the corners; he looked in the tack room.

"No horses?" I asked.

"No. No cattle or sheep either. We make our living raising racing Greyhounds, Mr. McNulty."

"Nice barn," I said.

"Thank you," Fard said. "It serves its purpose. Well, she

isn't here. I thought she was. She likes to wander sometimes. Let's try to see if we can't find her down by the river. She likes to watch the blue heron rookeries. I swear, if the dog were human, she would be a poet."

"Is that bad?" I asked. We seemed to be walking back to the house.

"I find it a little nebulous," Fard said.

"What grade are you in, Fard?"

"Sixth."

All the sixth graders I knew were a good foot taller than Fard. I'll bet they weren't a bit tougher, though. This kid talked funny; I couldn't put my finger on it. It certainly wasn't western. His diction seemed clipped. I had the feeling that if push came to shove, Fard could hold his own. We came to a stop at the front of my truck.

"Well, Fard, tell me about your godfather, Maddog McDermutt."

Fard tipped his Stetson up, looked at me, said: "What do you want to know?"

"I don't know. Anything, I guess. I only met him the night he gave me Jones. I don't know much about him. We've talked on the phone."

Jones stepped up to the WORTHINGTON mailbox and saluted it. As if it had a life of its own, the mailbox turned into a black swarm of flies. Jones' ears perked; surprised, he craned his neck; he stepped back. The swarm imploded, silenced; Jones blinked; he slowly lowered his leg, eyeing the mailbox warily. I laughed. "I had the same reaction," I said to Fard.

"That's not really our mailbox," Fard said. "I mean for letters and such. Our mailbox is up on the main road. This is

56

our old mailbox. Dad raises maggots in it. For whitefishing. He puts something dead in there, in this case a fox somebody had run over on the highway. Puts the fox in there, and voilà! Maggots!"

"Very creative," I said.

Now we seemed to be walking in the direction of the river. Jones moved on ahead into the cottonwoods.

"It is difficult to fathom, Mr. McNulty," Fard said, "how big and strong that Greyhound is. He truly is magnificent."

"Thank you, Fard. He can run a little, too."

"I'm almost sure he can, Mr. McNulty."

I paused, then had to ask: "Think your dog could take him, Fard?"

"Are you kidding?" Fard said. "Miss Neopolitan was solid Grade A. She won derbies."

I looked at Jones, out ahead of us, lifting his leg on a bush.

Fard continued: "Jones graded off at a cheap track. He couldn't make the turns. Jones couldn't win grade E. It was either find him a home or sell him to research or put him to sleep."

Jones perked his ears.

"No offense, Jones," Fard said, "but Miss Neopolitan could win Grade A races at the Great Falls track by about twenty lengths."

I thought about my big dog stretching out across the prairie; I had to wonder how Miss Neopolitan would have done with Jacques Ra....beet.

"You a betting man, Fard?" I asked. The last thing I would ever do is take a kid for money. But Fard was asking for it.

"You think your dog is faster than my dog, is that it?"

"I have to think so," I said. "I have to think my dog is faster."

"Well I'll tell you what we'll do," Fard said. "When Father arrives home, he can hold the two dogs. You and I will walk across the stubble for about a quarter of a mile; then we'll call the dogs. First dog reaches us, wins. What do you say?"

"You're on," I said.

"There she is," Fard said, pointing. And, indeed, a Greyhound lay under a cottonwood, staring up at a heron rookery. It did look like she was composing poetry. She saw Jones and stood up to greet him; both dogs wagged tails, sniffed noses, moved around to sniff ends as dogs do, then a snort, a push, a bolt, and they were off across the sandbar, through the cottonwoods, and off across the fields.

"Well?" I asked, my hand over my eyes, squinting.

"Well what?"

"Still think your Miss Neopolitan can take my Jones?"

"Mr. McNulty, I told you. Miss Neopolitan was one of the greatest Greyhounds in the Sport of Queens. She is older than your dog, you know. Even if your dog did beat my dog across the fields in a straight line, it wouldn't prove anything. We're talking about racing under the lights, wearing a racing blanket, wearing a racing muzzle, in front of a crowd, sitting in a jinny pit for hours, bumped and banged around by seven other dogs, maneuvering in tight quarters, breaking from starting boxes, living in a kennel situation."

Suddenly I felt terrible. I had been going on like a little kid who didn't know apples from sour grapes. My big brother can beat up your big brother. Fard, in spite of his age, was a Greyhound man. I was a school teacher. What I had was a giveaway Grade E reject, a candidate for laboratory research, a candidate for formaldehyde. Fard was right. I would love Jones no less if he could not outrun Miss Neopolitan. I did not care what grade Jones was or was not in. Grade A, Grade E, it made no difference. And Fard would lose no respect for his great Greyhound if Jones did outrun her across the field. So what was the point?

"I'm sorry, Fard," I said. "I was out of line."

We turned and started back for the house.

"They'll be back to the house before we are," Fard said. "Miss Neopolitan likes to run all the way to the neighbor fence, and that's about a quarter mile, then back across the flats to the barn."

"Tell me about Maddog," I said. "Like his name for instance."

"Well," Fard said, happy to change the subject, "legend has it Maddog was an Irish-Scotch cross, with some others thrown in, a German here, a Frenchman there, a little Greek way back, maybe, even, a slight trace of English. Fleas Finnegan argues that Maddog was not Irish-Scotch, but, in the main, Scotch-Irish. In this confusion the name McDermutt evolved to its present spelling. Originally, it was MacDourmouth. And his first name was Archibald. His middle name was Brewster. Archibald Brewster MacDourmouth."

Maybe I shouldn't have asked. Fard continued:

"And so MacDourmouth, McDermouth, Macdermud, McDermuck, you can see how the name evolved. Some genealogists insist that the name changed because the Macdourmouths from time to time needed a good alias, for example in times of financial stress, it was always helpful to have another name. Maddog insists that the MacDourmouth clan was not stupid, but merely ignorant, and nobody in the family could spell anything correctly, let alone the family name, and down through the ages it naturally changed on all the birth certificates and on all the family tombstones, until finally Maddog, some say, entered the great sport of dog racing with the name McDoughnutt. And when Archibald Brewster McDoughnutt ended up at the dog track with the likes of Fleas Finnegan, Pooch the Mooch McGill, Jake the Rake Smith, and Jake the Snake Johnson, and Little Elsie and Hugh Mungas, and Mangy Martinez, and Ben Dover, in no time at all, the name became McDermutt."

"I think I met all those people at the track," I said.

"I'm sure you did, Mr. McNulty. As I was saying, Fleas Finnegan started it. He took in on the McDoughnutt name something unmerciful, terrible and embarrassing to any who heard the teasing, and Finnegan, he had his returned in spades, but Maddog grew awful tired of Big Mac, and such, and ranging from Hey McNuggets, to would you like coffee with your McDoughnutt? And Maddog he would try, he would say like MacDourmouth, not McDoughnutt, and enunciate every syllable with extreme care, delicate, trippingly off the tongue, with a slight flair of Gaelic, but, nevertheless, as the years went by, the nutt became mutt, although many preferred nutt, and the dough became der, and McDermutt stuck. Some say it was because of the trace of German he had in him: der mutt."

Fard took a deep breath; he had not concluded:

"When you think about it MacDourmouth is not a far cry from McDermutt in the first place."

Now he had concluded. I mulled it over. The cameo of Maddog McDermutt reminded me of ninth grade essays: no beginning, no middle, no end.

"That is quite a story," I said.

"That's my middle name," Fard said.

"What is?"

"Maddog. My name is Fardington Maddog Worthington."

"Of course," I said. "It would be. I knew that. You told me that, that day you called me."

"I wonder what is keeping those two," Fard said. We walked by the whitefish-bait mailbox, and it came alive, turning into a black, buzzing cloud.

"You fish, Fard?" I said, ducking and stepping to the side of the cloud of flies.

"You bet," Fard said. "One day you will have to come fishing with Dad and me."

"I'd like to meet your dad," I said.

"Dad's not home. Neither is Mom."

"Well, I'm sorry I missed them. Perhaps another day."

"Of course." Fard looked out across the field. "That's odd," he said. "I wonder what's holding them up? Oh well. Would you like to come in while we wait?"

"Sure. Thanks."

Fard offered me a cup of coffee. I said, "Sure, Fard, great." While he was pouring, I stuck my head around the corner into the family room, and gasped.

I blinked. I blinked again.

Standing in the middle of the room was a Greyhound, dead as a coot, and stuffed. His two glass eyes were looking right at me.

"That's Mr. Inspiration," Fard said, coming alongside, handing me a cup of coffee. "He was the greatest Greyhound Dad ever owned. He died in a wreck on the first turn at West Palm Beach, broke his neck, and Dad had him sent to a taxidermist, and here he is. Before his accident, Dad had the lucky foresight to have his semen frozen. We think it was the first time anybody ever thought about artificial insemination with dogs, kind of a historic moment. When Miss Neopolitan comes in to season we plan to have her artificially inseminated to Mr. Inspiration. What do you think of that, Mr. McNulty?"

"I don't know what to think, Fard." I sipped my coffee. "How long has Mr. Inspiration been......stuffed?"

"I think twenty years."

Fard was at the window.

"Here come the dogs," he said.

I put my coffee down; we went out the door and down the walk. Jones and Miss Neopolitan came loping in the yard, tongues hanging out, rib cages rising and falling.

"Good run, Jones?" I asked. I patted him on the head.

Jones looked up, wagged his tail.

"Looks like they're smiling," Fard said. He patted his dog on the neck.

I nodded. Both dogs did look like they were smiling.

"Fard, I must be off. I thank you for the coffee and the company and meeting you and your fine Greyhound." I corrected myself. "Greyhounds," I said.

I reached down and scratched Miss Neopolitan on her pointed snout. She wagged her tail.

"Have you ever seen an unfriendly Greyhound?" I asked.

"No," Fard said. "Never have. There aren't any. You know, Mr. McNulty, the racing Greyhound is a superior animal. The irony is this: the breed has been ruthlessly culled for over 2,000 years. Like with other dogs in other registries, just because somebody's grandmother won a blue ribbon at a dog show means absolutely nothing when it comes to genetics. The proof is in the pudding. The racing Greyhound produces or ceases to exist. It's that simple. Because of the ruthless culling, the racing Greyhound is a superior animal, physically and mentally."

I looked at Jones. Physical, yes. Mental? He was no philosopher, I can tell you that much. Sally might even go further than that.

Jones jumped in the truck.

I climbed in the truck and closed the door.

"Good-bye, Mr. McNulty."

"Good-bye, Fard. Let's do this again some time."

I turned the truck around and drove onto the Ulm road, back through Ulm, onto I-15 and back to Great Falls. Jones sat up on the seat, leaning against the door, and continued to pant lightly. He seemed to be extremely content about life in general. I reached over and pushed the big guy on the shoulder. The dog growled at me; that was a first; it triggered the nightmare omen:

you, me, the dog

"What's the matter with you?" I asked. "You didn't run long or far enough to be that tired. You feel all right?"

Jones stared vacantly at the wheat fields going by.

SIX

I poured myself a half cup of coffee: black, hot, strong, same old battery acid. I dumped in three spoons of sugar, poured in half a cup of milk. I pulled up my chair, sipping. The last of the great hunters, Harry and Sheldon, had already found their places, ready to shoot the bull Third Period. In the position of new kid on the block, the new teacher in the school, I was so far behind I didn't know if I was afoot or horseback. I tried to use Third Period to my advantage: pre- pare, catch-up read the lit book, read the outside reading book, read papers, do grades, call a parent, help a kid if his study hall coincided. But not Harry and Sheldon. What they did with Third Period was blab on, on and on, like broken records, about their great hunting dogs. Day after day after day. Once in awhile, however, I managed to get in a good word about Jones.

For some unknown reason our principal, Dr. Mayonaisse, had become accustomed to making Third Period prep his period. He characteristically made his grand entrance about five minutes after the second bell. I moved the principal's stinky ashtray down the table.

"How you guys today?" I said, spreading my grade book,

lesson plan book, and a stack of papers around.

"Good good," Harry said.

"Great," Sheldon said. Today he had a saxophone lying on the table in front of him.

I saw that they had, as usual, no books, no papers, no homework. Must be nice. "I'll bet you guys are going to talk about your dogs," I said.

"You have something better to do?" Harry asked. "How's that overgrown track reject doing?"

"Jones is fine," I said. "Just fine."

I opened up my lesson plan book, not my all-time favorite modus operandi.

Fact is, I came to hate lesson plans either the first or second time I had to do them. Nobody I knew ever paid attention to lesson plans; I mean nobody; if that person existed, I had not found him or her yet; lesson plans were something I seemed to do because the department head tells you to because the principal told him to because the secondary superintendent told him to because the superintendent told him to because the school board thought it was wonderful because that's the way they do things in Minot, North Dakota. I was convinced there was absolutely no good reason on this round earth to have lesson plans, and everybody else agreed with me. Therefore: I wrote and turned in lesson plans.

As I put pen to paper and tried to have a thought worth having, Harry started in with his dog, Montana Black Satan, known in the field affectionately as, simply, Monty.

"Were you with me that time Monty went into the Missouri at forty below and pulled out seven honkers?" Harry asked Sheldon.

"Of course I was there. That was the time Bobo pulled

out seven honkers himself, and a mallard." Bobo, I happened to know, was short for Bobo the Great.

Harry looked Sheldon in the eye, and said: "I don't remember any mallard."

I looked up from my papers. Here he was. Right on schedule. Everybody's man of the hour. The boss! The principal!

Dr. Mayonaisse pulled back his folding chair with an ear-piercing scrape, plopped down, pulled himself up to the table, (I'd rather listen to a kid rake his nails along a blackboard), and proceeded to chain-smoke.

For the life of me, I don't know what his educational function was. He didn't do discipline; the deans did that. He didn't counsel anybody. The office secretaries did all the office work. The vice-principal made announcements, wrote bulletins, made out the schedules. I'd heard he observed new teachers from time to time, but he had yet to visit my classroom. Was I missing something? I know he didn't read my lesson plans, because anybody who did would say something, because my lesson plans did not make sense. Even to me they did not make sense. I highly suspected Dr. Mayonaisse could not read in the first place, anyway, but I made every effort to keep those dangerous ideas to myself. I could be wrong. About a week ago I took a pack of cigarettes off a kid, in my English class, because cigarettes on our Paris Gibson Junior High campus were absolutely taboo, a real priority no-no, wrote up the kid, turned in the cigarettes, turned in the kid. The next day I watched the principal smoke those same cigarettes. I stuck my head into my lesson plan book and tried to figure out what I would be doing Tuesday of next week, which really did not matter because the minute I wrote it down I would be off on something else, so I sat there and stared at the lesson plan book. Nothing was coming to mind.

Now Sheldon started in about how Bobo the Great had retrieved two Canadian honkers in the middle of white water rapids below Morony Dam in icy Missouri River water, and no other Irish setter would even think about that, in that Irish setters were usually considered upland bird dogs. Sheldon raved on and on about Bobo; Harry listened, and nodded, waited his turn to brag; I sat there, my nose stuck in my lesson plan book, the Third Period idiot, while the principal tried to turn himself into a charcoal briquette. The man appeared to be listening to Sheldon go on about Bobo the Great, but I don't think so. The doctor's eyes were too glazed over. Once in awhile he would grunt, or nod, or blow smoke straight up, inhaling deeply; then Sheldon would have to pause as Dr. Mayonaisse wretched. Sheldon went on for quite awhile about his Irish setter, about two cigarettes worth, judging from the dead sticks in the ash tray.

Then counter-point Harry, little devil's advocate Harry, he started up like a lawnmower engine on a cold day, on how he was duck hunting up at Freezeout, and the first of the snow geese had arrived and how Montana Black Satan who everybody called Monty retrieved not only his geese, and his ducks, but everybody else's ducks and geese, and to hear him tell it, there must have been 500 people in that blind, and that black lab, the greatest breed of water dog in the world, retrieved 'em all and wanted to stay for more, even though the temperature was below zero, and the dog had to frequently break ice. I gave the edge to Harry, because now five butts stared at us from the ash tray.

Occasionally, throughout these canine discussions, the principal gagged and coughed on his own smoke, muttered

68

something about some kid's mother, or bad-mouthed a counselor with some administrative jargon I never did catch, (he blubbered), smashed his butt in an ashtray, ground it around good, stared at it awhile, then suddenly stood up, brushed himself off, as if filled with inspiration, like it had finally come upon him what he was supposed to be doing, and rushed out the room. I wasn't sure, but I don't think the man knew who I was. He never said hello or good-bye, and this was no exception.

I stuck my nose in my lesson plan book.

"Can your racing Greyhound swim?" Harry asked.

"What's that?"

"Your dog. Can he swim?"

"I presume so."

"Does he hunt?" Sheldon asked.

"Don't you guys ever do lesson plans?" I asked. "Am I a stupid Lone Ranger? I have a terrible time with these blasted lesson plans."

"I teach orchestra," Sheldon said, turning his saxophone over.

"Well, how do you know what you will be doing next Thursday, for example?"

"I teach orchestra," Sheldon said.

"I wrote mine five years ago," Harry explained. "I change the date and turn in a facsimile."

"You haven't changed your methods in five years?"

"Well, of course I have," Harry said "Nobody reads those things. I don't read them. I turn them in. You remember old Ed Fixter retired three years ago? Nah. I suppose that's before your time. Williams up in 302 turns Fixter's plans in, every week."

I thought about it.

"What if I turned in one of yours?"

"Fine with me," Harry said. "Write your name at the top, turn it in."

I closed my lesson plan book. "You're on," I said.

Sheldon and Harry exchanged glances, grinned.

"So does that dog of yours hunt?" Sheldon asked again.

"No. Not really. Jones and I go for walks almost every day. Once in awhile a rabbit jumps up and Jones chases it."

"I'll bet that's something to see," Sheldon said.

"He gets after it," I said.

"How fast can he go?" Harry asked.

"I'm not sure," I said. "You know I read somewhere that they had a race between a man, a dog, and a horse, in Phoenix I think." I paused to let that sink in. "The man was the quickest, then the dog, then the horse. Then, on the other end of it, like a 100 mile race, the man is also the strongest. The horse and dog will break down. The man, if his feet don't fail, keeps plugging along."

We sipped our battery acid. The boys were looking me over.

"Furthermore," I said, pressing on, "the racing Greyhound is a superior animal. The breed, you know, has been ruthlessly culled for over 2,000 years. Just because your Montana Black Satan had a grandmother in a big dog show, or just because Bobo the Great's second cousin won a beauty contest means absolutely nothing when it comes to genetics. The proof is in the pudding. The racing Greyhound is a superior animal, physically and mentally."

Harry and Sheldon just looked at me.

Had I won new respect? I sipped my battery acid. I had to

admit, I would rather talk about my dog Jones and Greyhounds than write meaningless lesson plans. I was afraid it could become a habit.

"Those Greyhounds good for anything except running?" Harry asked.

"Sure. Jones is very attentive; he's very lovable; he is sensitive to instructions; I suspect he is a good watchdog although I don't know for sure on that. He's clean. He's gentle. He's loyal. There is no question he is my dog. What more could you ask for?"

Harry leaned forward, eyeball to eyeball, and said: "Well yeah, but he doesn't do anything, as such, is what I meant."

Sheldon helped out: "What Harry's getting at, if your Greyhound can't hunt birds, he's not good for much at all."

"Jones knows what a bird is," I said. "I'll bet he could be a fine bird dog. He's smart. He'd pick it up fast."

"We're going out for pheasant Saturday morning," Harry said. "Want to come along?"

"Saturday morning? Sure, why not."

"What do you shoot?" Sheldon asked.

"I don't have a gun."

"Then you can watch us show you how it's done," Harry said. "How would you like to watch two of the best pheasant dogs this side of the Mississippi, and this side of the Rocky Mountains, work the upper Missouri River breaks?"

"Sure," I said. "Why not?"

We met about six miles out of town, up the river, on the east side. I pulled the truck into the wide spot, next to Harry's truck and behind Sheldon's truck, turned the key, leaned over and opened Jones's door, and he jumped easily down and ran off into the trees.

71

Sheldon was aghast.

"Call your dog!" he hissed. "He'll scare everything away."

"That dog is going to ruin everything," Harry said.

"Jones!" I yelled. "Here Jones!"

We heard some branches snap. Some thrashing. Big branches snapping. Crashing. A deer burst from the brush, bounded across the road and up the coulee, then another, then two more, then another, three more.

"There's a whole herd of 'em in there!" Harry said.

"You mean there was," Sheldon said.

We all heard the dog bark.

"Jones!" I yelled. "Here Jones! Here boy!"

We heard more breaking branches, frantic honking from the river, a thrashing and beating of wings on water, and at least fifty honkers were running along the top of the river, trying to go airborne. What a racket they made. Then a flock of quacking mallards took off. Five blue herons came up off the river bank and flapped off.

"Cripes," Harry said. "We're through here. We better move on."

A ring-neck pheasant burst from the brush, on the run across the field, headed for the coulee. We could hear the struggles of Jones crashing through the brush, a yelp of pain, stepped on something maybe, or slapped by a branch, then a bark of pure pleasure, more crashing.

The pheasant was airborne now, pumping hard, in a big hurry, but he was not catching any helping updraft. From between two clumps of bushes, like they were gates on a starting box slamming open, burst my big Greyhound Jones, and he was charging, head down, low to the ground; he meant to have that pheasant. Harry's big lab took it all in and went into a beautiful point. Sheldon's Irish setter took three steps forward, up went the leg, out went the tail. Beautiful. Two disciplined statues. Jones was closing fast. Harry and Sheldon brought their shotguns around, leading the pheasant. "No!" I cried. "Don't shoot! You'll hit my dog!"

The pheasant reached the borrow pit; Jones leaped; Jones had the pheasant in mid air, bouncing to a stop, throwing gravel around with his feet, nails digging in; then he lost his balance and tripped, end over end, buns over teakettles, to vanish into the adjacent borrow pit.

Harry and Sheldon lowered their shotguns. The Irish setter and black lab remained on point. I had the distinct impression the boys were not real thrilled.

We waited.

In a moment, Jones trotted up out of the borrow pit, crossed the road, pheasant in mouth, sat down in front of me. I took the pheasant. "Thank you, Jones. Well done."

Harry and Sheldon looked the pheasant over, poking around in the beautiful feathers, peering in. "I'll be," Harry said. "A soft-mouthed Greyhound. The bird doesn't have a mark on him."

"What do I do now?" I asked, holding fast to the beautiful creature. "Turn him loose so you can blast him?"

The pheasant cocked a black, beady eye to Harry, as if he understood my remark. The bird looked very much like a streamlined chicken, dressed up for Mardi Gras.

"That's hardly sporty," Harry said.

"Your dogs are going to cramp," I said. They were still on point, twisted around, front legs up, tails out, faces puzzled

73

at this new hunting technique. They never took their eyes off the pheasant.

"Well," Sheldon said, "usually when we see a pheasant we shoot, then the dogs retrieve. You're not supposed to turn your stupid dog loose and make the whole river bottoms crazy. You might as well have driven a freight train through there."

"Well excuse me," I said. "I seem to be the one with the pheasant."

"Yeah, right," Harry said. He picked up his black lab and put him in his truck. The dog stood on the truck seat, continuing to point, more stone than flesh and blood.

"Is he all right?" I asked.

"He'll recover," Harry said.

Sheldon called his Irish setter, who seemed to have developed a tick in his right eye; the dog perked an ear, then relaxed, then jumped in Sheldon's truck.

"Grab Jones there, will you?" I asked, and Harry grabbed the dog's collar. I turned loose the ring-neck. He took off on the run, went airborne, this time he caught an updraft and he soared over the trees and over the river. We all watched him go. That lucky bird had something to tell his grandchickees.

I grabbed Jones's collar, then stuffed the big guy in my truck, up on the seat, and shut the door. "I think I'll call it a day," I said. "You always want to leave something for seed. I'm going to head on back to town. You fellas have a good day."

Monday, Third Period prep was the usual. Harry and Sheldon went at it tooth and nail about whose dog performed best, about this shot, or that point, or the one that got away

74

for some reason or another. The principal sat there, smoking away, oblivious. When Sheldon and Harry retold the part about my dog catching the pheasant unassisted, up and ran it down, the principal joined the conversation.

"What kind of dog do you have, Bill?"

"Ryan, Dr. Mayonaisse. My name is Ryan."

"That's all right, too. What kind?"

"Greyhound."

"You know," he said, "I read in the paper the other day about Greyhounds. The military, the army I think, was using racing Greyhound rejects for research. They break the dogs' legs, then replace the damage with plastic."

I had already heard that one from Maddog, but I said: "That's awful."

The principal looked over the saxophone, like it was the first time he had noticed it. "What's that?" he asked.

"A saxophone," Sheldon said.

"Of course it is," Dr. Mayonaisse said. He paused a moment, then added, "What's it do?"

Sheldon said, "Well, in the case of this saxophone, not much. It spent the summer in Holter Lake and everything is rusted shut. Nothing works."

"I see." Dr. Mayonaisse looked at his watch, then ground out his cigarette. "That reminds me," he said. "I have to be somewhere."

At the door, he paused, and said, to me: "Don't forget to turn in your lesson plans."

The bell rang ending Third Period.

SEVEN

The ten mile drive to Ulm from Great Falls took only twenty minutes, now that I knew where Fard lived. I parked the truck in front of the WORTHINGTON mailbox. Sally stepped out her side, on the mailbox side; I stepped out my side. Jones sat in the middle of the truck, looking to one door, then the other, like let's see now, which side should I choose, and I said, "Get your lazy buns out the truck, Jones," and he jumped out Sally's side.

"Why are all those flies buzzing around that mailbox?" Sally asked, flailing away at the great black swarm.

"Fard's dad raises maggots for whitefishing," I explained.

"Of course I should have known," Sally muttered. "It should have been obvious. Everybody raises maggots in their mailbox. It's a status symbol."

As Sally and I walked up the sidewalk, Jones rushed on ahead to check out a shrub, then saluted it as I knocked on the screen door which rattled and crashed in the door jam.

In a moment the door opened; Fard stood there, smiling.

"Mr. and Mrs. McNulty. And Jones. How nice to see you. Please. Won't you all come in?"

I held Jones by the collar as Sally went in first. I released Jones; he lumbered on in. The screen door slammed shut, all on its own, behind me.

"You sure you want Jones in the house?" I asked.

"Oh sure," Fard said. "Miss Neopolitan comes in the house whenever she feels like it. And Mr. Inspiration is in the house all the time, as you know. Mom and Dad are out in the barn. Would you like a glass of lemonade, or a cookie, or something, before we go out to watch the whelping? You're in time. We're going to have puppies any minute now."

I was about to say no thanks to the lemonade and cookie when I noticed the hair on Jones's neck and back stand up. Like about an inch the hair stood up. I hadn't seen that before. He growled, then whined, then growled some more.

Sally pointed, said: "There's a Greyhound in the living room."

"Oh that's Mr. Inspiration," Fard said. "He was the fastest dog that ever lived. Father had him stuffed."

Sally said, to me, under her breath, "Talk about macabre."

"Shhhhh," I hissed. "Don't be rude."

"Bizarre," Sally hissed back. "Strictly bizarre. Maggots in the mailbox and a stuffed dog in the living room?"

We all seemed to mosey into the living room.

"Mr. Inspiration," I said, trying to be chipper, "looks like he is watching television."

Fard chuckled. "We faced him that way on purpose, Mr. McNulty. We all felt it gave him something to do."

"How thoughtful," Sally said. "What's this little shelf on the dog's side for?"

I walked around to check it out. Sure enough, on the side of Mr. Inspiration, stapled to his side, was a little shelf.

Fard explained. "Mom and Dad put their drinks there when

they watch television."

I thought about it. "Why not," I said, attempting a grin.

Sally said, "Have to put your drinks somewhere, eh? Might as well make the dog useful. Some dogs get your slippers. Some dogs go out and get the paper. This dog holds your drinks."

Jones walked over to Mr. Inspiration, stiff-legged, humped up like a big Halloween cat, the hair on his neck and back standing straight up, his ears straight up, his eyes big and non-blinking, his tail stuck straight out like Harry or Sheldon's bird dogs on the point. Jones growled.

"Stop that, Jones," I said. "Be a good dog."

Jones stepped back, took a bow, put his head on his paws, his butt stuck up in the air; his tail waved back and forth; he barked.

"No Jones," I said.

He barked again.

"Stop it, Jones."

Jones barked.

"I mean it, Jones."

Jones ran around Mr. Inspiration and took a long, studious whiff under the stuffed dog's tail. He ran back to look the dog in a glass eye. Nothing. No response. Oh well, I thought, no harm done. I glanced at Sally and smiled. I did find the whole thing somewhat amusing.

Jones barked, bit playfully at the dog's nose.

"Jones, stop that," I said.

Jones barked again, then barked yet again at his shoulder.

"All right, Jones, that's enough."

Jones poked Mr. Inspiration along the rib cage, sniffed the underside stem to stern, looking up once at me, from under Mr. Inspiration's belly button, then suddenly, with no warning whatsoever, Jones reared up on his hind legs, came down with all his weight on the dog's back, and you could hear the spine crack, and it was awful and made your teeth itch to hear it, and Jones knocked the stuffed dog clean off his little pedestal, breaking the doweling that held the dog in place, over on his side, then on his back, the feet and legs stuck straight up, then Jones took a bite out of the midsection, below the sternum, and Mr. Inspiration made a popping sound, something like a "pop-ping-pop," like a banjo string breaking against the head, and Jones ripped and tore and out of Mr. Inspiration popped what looked like Styrofoam and cotton and straw as well as three wires which went "ping, ping, ping," maybe a little anti-climactic.

It happened fast.

"How quaint," Sally said.

Fard seemed speechless. He stood there, bow-legged, under his cowboy hat, both thumbs tucked to either side of his chrome belt buckle engraved F.A.R.D.

"Oh no," I said, feeling my face flush, growing ashamed, leaping across Mr. Inspiration and grabbing Jones by the collar. "Let go, Jones!"

Jones growled, then dug in deeper. Mr. Inspiration's neck was coming apart at the shoulder. The fawn hide ripped and cracked like an old piece of leather.

"Jones!" I shouted. "Stop that! No! Bad dog!"

At times like this I wished he wasn't so big. The power of the dog was insurmountable.

Jones picked up the mangled dummy dog and threw it across the room. Mr. Inspiration hit the wall, one back leg bent back, and you could hear it snap on impact, and it crumpled like it was broken in about seventeen places, and the dog landed on its head, back broken, neck broken, leg broken, and straw, Styrofoam, cotton and three wires poking out the stomach. No question. Jones had ruined an absolutely fine stuffed Greyhound, in my judgment, beyond repair.

"Well done, Jones," I said. "Thank you much for a monumental damage bill."

I held Jones by the collar, feeling sicker by the moment.

Fard said, "Mom and Dad won't be too happy about that."

Fard went to Mr. Inspiration, picked the dog up, tried to remold what was left, and somehow, bless his heart, made the thing stand up, but Mr. Inspiration was not the same dog. Jones had rearranged everything, looked like to me. Nobody, even in a drunken stupor, would recognize this dog as in anything but very tough shape.

I felt like I should say something. "Maybe we could run a pin through that shelf and drill a hole in the floor, instead of having the dog hold up the shelf, have the shelf hold up the dog, if you grab my meaning."

"Bizarre," Sally said. "Really bizarre."

The dog wouldn't stand, the broken leg and broken back going goosie, and he fell over on his side, one glass eye falling out of its socket when the head slammed to the floor, and the eye rolled like a marble under a chair.

Jones growled and lunged at Mr. Inspiration.

"Stop that, Jones!" I said. "Stop it."

Jones growled at me!

"Geeze," I said, "what's with you?"

"Is that taxidermy stuff expensive?" I asked Fard, pulling Jones back. "Let go, you idiot," I said, twisting the collar, cutting off his air. Jones reluctantly released his hold on Mr.

Inspiration, but not before he broke the stuffed dog's leg.

"I think so," Fard said, setting the Greyhound up, trying to balance it on two legs, and he did. Bless his heart, he actually did. The Greyhound actually stood there. As Fard stepped back to judge his work, some straw fell out the stomach and onto the floor. "Let's hope Father can fix it. Shall we retire to the whelping barn?"

"Sure. You bet," I said, dragging Jones out the room. "You fool," I said to the dog. "No not you, Fard, I was talking to this worthless dog." We all filed out the house.

Shortly after the screen door slammed shut, I could hear the stuffed dog fall thud to the floor again. I hoped Fard's parents had a sense of humor. I guessed maybe that might not be the case. Canine idolatry? Mutt worship? A dog shrine? A family heirloom of dog races gone by? Why didn't they bury the dog and be done with it? Life is for the living. Small wonder Jones found the stuffed dog offensive.

"Your dad likes to fish, eh Fard?" Sally said, nodding to the WORTHINGTON mailbox, the swarm rising right on schedule.

"Oh most certainly, Mrs. McNulty. I presume Mr. McNulty told you we raise maggots in a dead fox in there."

"He neglected to mention the dead fox."

We stepped into the barn.

"You're in time," a voice said. My eyes adjusted to the darker lighting of the barn. Two figures were seated around a bed of straw on which lay the fawn-colored, swollen-bellied Miss Neopolitan, whom Jones and I had met two months ago.

"Father," Fard said, "I would like you to meet Mr. and Mrs. McNulty. Mr. McNulty is a school teacher in Great Falls."

Mr. Worthington grunted, like it was a great strain to stand up, but he made it, and we shook hands. He was my height. "Nice to meet you," he said, leaning forward, and my head reeled from the blast of whiskey off the man's breath. I looked more closely at Mr. Worthington, top to bottom. No hat, balding. Hadn't shaved in several days. Maybe hadn't slept in days. Overalls dirty, no...filthy, over what looked like faded pink underwear. And clodhopper boots with straw and stuff stuck to the sides. Back to the man's face, his complexion reminded me of a big city road map, streets, freeways, alleys, avenues, all crisscrossing and intersecting, and his nose, in particular, very striking, bulbous, looked like a piece of pottery didn't cook well in the kiln, cracked every which way but still in one piece. Judging from the man's breath, he very well might be 100 proof, a walking, talking pickle. Mr. Worthington stepped sideways to shake Sally's hand. "Nice to meet you," he slurred.

I felt that I should mention the stuffed dog in the house, and the unfortunate accident, just somehow start right in, but I seemed to be stuck on the launch pad.

"And I would like you to meet my mother," Fard said. "Mother, these are the McNultys."

And around we went, something of a repeat performance. Fard's mother grunted, stood up, wiped her hands on her overalls, also over what appeared to be faded red underwear, and shook Sally's hand. I had had the passing thought I would be better off trying to explain what had happened in the Worthington living room to a female ear, perhaps with a little more understanding, a little more sympathy, a little more empathy, but one look at Mrs. Worthington, and I'm afraid that idea went down the drain. After shaking hands with Sally,

Mrs. Worthington globbed on to my hand, leaned forward, and said, "Nice to meet you," and I about passed out. I think the woman had been drinking gasoline. I hoped she did not smoke, because if she did and lit up, the fumes from her breath would blow her head right off her neck. I said, "Nice to meet you, Mrs. Worthington," and put my hand to my mouth to fight back a gag. If Mr. Worthington's nose was a focal point of physiognomy, Mrs. Worthington's hair was certainly worth mentioning. I know of junior high girls who would give their monthly allowance to know what Mrs. Worthington did to her hair to have it stand straight up like that. Her hair, something of a brunette I think, hard to tell in the barn light, stood straight up, a good foot, and out in all directions, another good foot. Even in that dark barn, it was something to behold. They didn't build a comb that'd take a run at that permanent. Mrs. Worthington sat down next to the dog. I glanced at Sally. I had to wonder what she'd do with hair like that.

"And," Fard said, "this is Miss Neopolitan, named after the ice cream, not the general. I believe you have met," he said, indicating me. I nodded. Then Fard concluded his introductions, pointing to Jones: "Mother. Father. This is the McNulty dog Jones, the one Godfather Maddog McDermutt gave away on the closing of the Great Falls track."

I nodded. Enough said on that subject.

"He's a big one, ain't he?" Mr. Worthington observed. "I've always been an advocate of finding homes for the worthless worse than Grade E dogs. They do make nice pets."

"Lovely," Sally said, winking at Jones.

"Jones is more than a pet," I said. "And he is hardly worthless." Then I remembered Mr. Inspiration. "But you never know," I said, adding, "he could very well be worthless, I agree."

Jones stepped forward to touch noses with Miss Neopolitan.

"Looks like they remember each other," Fard said. "Golly, it's been two months hasn't it?"

"Almost to the day," I said.

Jones then wandered off to a corner of the barn, selected a patch of straw, went around and around and around, and plopped himself down to watch, from a distance, the proceedings, cried out in surprise, stood up, sniffed at the straw, barked at it.

"Now what?" I said, going over to my dog. I saw what was bothering him. Jones had sat on the Worthington bottle.

"Help yourself," Mr. Worthington said.

"No thanks," I said.

"Well, toss it over," he said. "I could stand a pull. Isn't every day my dog has pups."

I picked up the bottle, handed it over. Mr. Worthington pulled the cork, swallowed three times, handed it over to Mrs. Worthington who almost drained it. She corked it and set it to one side. I smiled pleasantly at Sally. I think I was feeling a little silly from the fumes.

Fard stepped forward and dropped to his knees. He patted Miss Neopolitan on the neck, then gently down the side, stopping at her bloated stomach. "There's one!" Fard said. "I could feel the little fellow that time. How many pups you think she has in there?"

Fard's father answered: "Quite a few."

"Is not mother nature a magnificent phenomenon?" Fard asked all around.

"Yes," I said. "Miraculous. Thanks for inviting us out."

"We Greyhound people have to stick together," Fard said.

Sally and I nodded, smiled pleasantly.

Mrs. Worthington belched.

Fard continued: "Bred in the purple. These pups are without question bred in the purple. Mr. Inspiration and Miss Neopolitan. What a cross. Some people in the dog business would kill for those bloodlines. Would you agree with that assessment, Father?"

Jones started cleaning himself up so loudly over on his straw bed, I had to shush him.

"Jones! Stop that," I hissed.

The dog stared back, like what was my problem.

"Clean yourself later," I said. Then, to Sally, I added, "He's becoming a little brassy all the way around."

Sally nodded

Polite nods all around anyway. Understanding nods. Dog people nods. Dogs will be dogs.

what you need, McNulty, is a dog

"Would you like to sit down?" Mrs. Worthington said.

"That's fine," Sally said. "We do have another engagement and can't stay too long."

"Father," Fard said, "I told a couple of the kids on the school bus you paid five hundred bucks to keep sperm frozen from that famous dog our famous dog associate, that one and only dog trainer, and everybody knows who he is, sent us lots of years back, and that dog who is still with us today, if he was alive he'd be twenty-two years old, standing proud as the day he won the derby, stuffed by the greatest taxidermist the world has ever known, and today and forever stands mounted in our living room as a testament to his greatness, or at least he did, and how the vet in Great Falls artificially inseminated the great Miss Neopolitan, named after the ice cream, not the general, not once but twice, with sperm frozen and kept by us in our own ice box, and what a remarkable scientific accomplishment all that was, and Brad Thompson and John Rogers, they were really impressed. Brad, he said they take their bitch over to Fort Benton, and John, he said his uncle had a Chinese Chow Chow and his uncle even brings the stud to them, so they had trouble with this frozen stuff, and it'd be terrible if anything ever happened to Mr. Inspiration, but there is one thing we have to tell you."

I felt my Adam's apple go up and stick there.

"Then I told the same two kids," Fard said, reaching out to pat his pregnant Greyhound, "what great bloodlines Mr. Inspiration carries, and what a great cross we will have with Miss Neopolitan, and how much money we're going to make running the pups in the kennel of the great Maddog McDermutt, my godfather."

"Did you see the great Mr. Inspiration?" Mr. Worthington asked.

I cleared my throat. "Yes," I said, and it came out something like a croak, "as a matter of fact we did."

"Here we go!" Fard's father said.

"I really do apologize," I muttered, but nobody heard me.

"Wow!" Fard said, his eyes wide.

A pup was on the way. Miss Neopolitan labored down hard. She grunted. She pushed. The bag broke. She relaxed. Fard was right there. His mother grabbed Fard by the shoulder and jerked him away. "Give the dog a little breathing room, Son," she said. "Miss Neopolitan knows what she is doing."

I glanced at Jones. He was cleaning himself again.

"I'll say," Fard said. "I should say she does."

Fard grabbed a shovel and talked into it, pretending it was a microphone, mimicking a track announcer, his voice going falsetto. "The dogs are coming out onto the track." And here he inserted his version of a trumpet call of the dogs to the track on which I stood to think he could practice a little.

Fard's mother explained: "Fard's father had taken Fard to the dog track on several occasions, once in Rapid City, once to Mile High, once to Multnomah, and so he knows all that track stuff."

"And out of the starting boxes, racing in the Great One's Kennel at Rapid City in front of thousands and thousands of Greyhound fans, it's the derby, it's the race of the year, it's the race everybody has been waiting for, and breaking first, it is........." Fard paused. "We're going to have to come up with some names?"

"All in good time," Fard's father said. "All in good time."

The first pup had been born. Gray brindle! The mother grunted, and lifted her head and shoulders, and reached around to lick the pup. The pup squealed.

"Hooray!" Fard said.

Nods all around.

"Isn't that the cutest little puppy," Sally said.

"Here comes number two," Fard's mother said.

And Fard picked up his shovel and said, in his best falsetto, "and going in to the first turn we have another dog making a challenging run at the leader of the pack, that bred-in-the-purple Mr. Inspiration and Miss Neopolitan, and here it comes, and here it comes, and yes it is, what a dog race, we have another gray brindle going for the big win."

Miss Neopolitan lifted her head and shoulders to lick the

88

second pup. Mrs. Worthington picked up the first born. "It's a boy," she said, setting him back down.

Fard picked up the same pup and looked him over. "Sure is," he said.

"Where's that gray brindle coming from?" Pa asked.

I glanced at Jones. He was watching now, curious. A pup squealed; Jones' ears perked.

The second pup squealed and squirmed, and Miss Neopolitan picked it up, brought it forward, where she could work on it with less effort. "Don't forget this guy," Fard said. And he picked up the first-born and placed it next to the second-born and Miss Neopolitan cleaned up the both of them. Blind, helpless, clumsy, squealy, the pups bumped and shoved and pushed.

"Notice the pup looks like a bulldog," Fard said.

"Perfectly normal," his father said, his voice full of knowledge and wisdom. "Puppy Greyhounds have noses like that. It'll be awhile before the next one is born, more than likely. Dog has two chutes. Pup comes down chute number one; second pup comes down chute number two. Then we wait awhile for the next two."

"You sure are downright unquestionably all-time knowledgeable about whelping Greyhounds, Father. Did you learn about dogs and in particular racing Greyhounds with my godfather Maddog McDermutt, the greatest dog trainer of all time?"

"Well, some maybe," his father modestly had to admit.

"Well Father," Fard said, "I think maybe you might be mistaken, because here comes Number Three." Fard picked up his shovel. "And going by the backstretch in front of the tote board...."

"Oh shut your mouth," Fard's mother said. I gave her the school teacher "I understand" look, as she continued: "Don't make a bigger fool out of yourself than you already are."

Fard pointed to Miss Neopolitan, said, "Here comes number four."

"I love a consistent litter," Pa said. "It's a wonderful sign. It truly is. When all the dogs are similar, there's a marvelous chance they'll all be great. I had a hunch on this one; I surely did."

"Solid Grade A Litter, eh Father?" Fard said.

"They look like clones," Mr. Worthington said. "All gray brindle. Same markings." Mr. Worthington gave Jones a long, studious look, then back to the pups.

"Are gray brindle puppies unusual out of two fawns?" I asked.

"Unusual?" Mr. Worthington said. "I thought it was impossible."

"Boy," Fard said. "Mr. Inspiration really pulled a neat trick there, huh Dad?"

"Maybe their parents were brindle," I suggested. "And it's coming through now. A throwback or something."

Jones stood up, stretched, yawned, and walked out of the barn.

"I don't think so," Mr. Worthington said, patting the mother dog on the neck.

Miss Neopolitan thumped her tail. The four pups were finding their way to the faucets.

"Oh look," Fard said, rubbing his chin thoughtfully. "What do we have forthcoming now?"

Fard, his father, his mother, Sally and I all stared intently at the pup trying to make its way in to the world.

Plop!

And Miss Neopolitan was up and at it, cleaning it up, picking it up, licking it, and the pup whined, then growled.

Fard's father spoke first: "What..........is that?"

"Odd-looking Greyhound," Fard said. He picked it up and everybody took a gander. This pup was gray, like the others, but not brindle by any means. It had LONG HAIR. Its tail was hairy. Really hairy. And he wasn't built like the others. This one was rangier, if that was possible. His paws were broader, thicker.

After awhile Fard's father took a stab at it: "You know what that looks like?"

Everybody shrugged. I sure didn't know.

"That pup," Fard's father said, "looks like a wolf. I swear, that pup looks like a wolf."

"A wolf!" Fard said and quickly set the pup back down like it was a hot potato. Miss Neopolitan picked it up and set it by the others.

"Throwback?" Fard's mother asked.

"That's some throw," Mr. Worthington said. "I'd be more inclined to go with a mutation theory."

"What's the gestation period on a Greyhound?" I asked.

Fard answered: "Sixty-two days."

Two months.

"I paid a lot of money to have that stud dog's sperm frozen," Mr. Worthington said

"Maybe we froze it too much," Fard suggested. The hairy pup crawled in with the rest of the litter. It was a tender moment, I thought, all around, no question.

"Maybe the hair will fall off in time," Fard suggested, pointing to indicate the newborn puppy. "You know, like baby teeth."

"Here we go again," Fard's father said.

"Wow," Fard said. "Big litter. I guess she didn't pack 'em in chute by chute on that last one, huh Father?"

"Thank God," Mr. Worthington said, looking once again at the odd-looking pup.

Miss Neopolitan was dropping another pup.

It looked like the first four.

Everybody cheered.

"Shh," Fard's mother said. "We're upsetting Miss Neopolitan."

"She ain't done, yet," Mr. Worthington said.

Miss Neopolitan took care of each pup, licking a back, a neck, a bottom, moving on to the next when satisfied, then Fard offered her some water. She lapped at the pan of water, then lay her head down on the straw to relax for a moment.

Another was coming into the world.

The folks stared at the next pup.

Finally, Fard said, "That's no wolf."

"Now what we got going on this time?" Fard's father finally said.

"If you want to know what I think," Fard said, "that pup bears a striking similarity to John Rogers' Chinese Chow Chow Chi Ki Pow. He surely does."

"If that miserable Chinese Chow Chow got around my blue blood here, I am going to have a conniption fit."

"Wish you wouldn't," Mrs. Worthington said. "Last conniption fit you had none of us ever want to see again. Now settle down. Your neck is bright red. Your cheeks are puffed. Your eyes are starting to bug. You take it easy. There's some real nice Greyhounds in there and there is not one bit of Chinese Chow Chow or wolf in them. Take a slug off your bottle there."

Mr. Worthington finished it off.

"Here comes another one," Sally said.

"Oh look," Fard said, "It looks like the other one."

"Two Chinese Chow Chows!" Mr. Worthington said.

"Five Greyhounds, a wolf, and two Chinese Chow Chows," I summarized, nodding and grinning at everyone. "That's remarkable."

At this time old man Worthington had his promised conniption fit. The lines in the man's face turned redder; the bulbous nose seemed to swell under pressure, like it wanted to explode. He marched from the barn, fists clenched at his side.

"I better call the sheriff," Mrs. Worthington said, grunting on the rise, following along after Mr. Worthington.

Fard sat down next to the litter of puppies, reached over and patted Miss Neopolitan, patted the puppies. "Could be bad," he said.

I bent over and scratched Miss Neopolitan's ear. "Maybe we ought to be moving along," I said. "Fard, will you be all right?"

"Oh sure, Mr. McNulty, and thank you for dropping out."

Fard picked up the wolf and turned him over, and over, then put him back on a faucet.

He muttered, "Maybe now those smart-alecky airheads at Cascade Grade School in the sixth grade, music class, back row, will believe me when I said I saw a wolf couple of months back. Little feller, I bet you could be one mean bugger in a dog fight when you grow up."

It was an interesting thought.

"Trouble is," he said to the litter in general, "you're all

supposed to be Greyhounds. Darned if I can figure it out."

I stood up and whispered to Sally. "It's what they call a split litter," I said.

"Two different fathers?" she said.

"Looks to me like three," I said.

Fard arose. "I'd better go inside," he said to the mother and pups. "If you'll excuse me, Mr. and Mrs. McNulty." Fard headed for the house.

Jones met us at the barn door.

"Come on, Jones," I said, and we walked to the truck.

Mrs. Worthington came down the walk, followed by Fard, past the WORTHINGTON mailbox which erupted into a fine black cloud. She informed us: "That stupid sheriff didn't understand me when I told him the old man's racing Greyhound had a wolf and two Chinese Chow Chows and he was so upset he went after John's dad with a baseball bat and Lord knows who else and what the sheriff eventually wanted to know is if the wolf bit your father, and I said no it was a baby, and he said it doesn't matter rabies is rabies, and then he said your father was mad, and I said no kidding why did you think I called, and before I could hang up the sheriff was hollering to his deputy we had a rabid dog loose and get the car, and he hung up."

I could hear a siren in the distance.

From the living room Mr. Worthington screamed: "What happened to Mr. Inspiration?"

Fard said, "Dad doesn't have rabies. He doesn't even have distemper."

An agonizing wail from inside the house: "What happened to my dog!"

I could not ignore my obligations any longer. I walked up

94

the sidewalk, in the house, stepped in to the living room. "Well sir," I began....I stopped. The man had a baseball bat. And it looked like he knew how to use it.

Mr. Worthington was looking at Jones, who had joined me, standing at my side. The man pointed his bat at the dog. "That dog is gray brindle."

"Yes sir," I said. "He surely is. He's as gray brindle a Greyhound as I've ever seen."

The man thumped his bat on the floor

"Fard," old man Worthington said, "you said that dog was out here two months ago?"

Fard stuck his head in the living room, said, "Well yes, but...."

"Please don't point that bat at my dog," I said. "You can not hold us responsible for the snag, or should I say snags, in Miss Neopolitan's litter to the frozen sperm of," and I pointed to the ruined Mr. Inspiration, "that dog there."

I thought that I had made that point rather well and took a moment to let it sink in.

I continued: "Somehow, a wolf and two Chinese Chow Chows are involved in this incident, and apparently none of the Greyhound pups should have been gray brindle, but you can hardly hold anybody other than your dog out there in the barn responsible."

Worthington became unglued.

He raised his bat and started swinging it in circles around his head, grunting and moaning primordial noises, and his road-map face grew bright red, all the little roads and avenues and streets meshing into one big red blotch, and his throat became swollen, and his eyes bugged out.

It was awful to see and hear.

Old man Worthington went on about the loose morals of wolves and Chinese Chow Chows, because a dog like Miss Neopolitan, whom he had raised himself and could vouch, personally, as to her morals, would not throw herself around like that and lower herself to a non-Greyhound status, especially with Mr. Inspiration's bloodlines available in the freezer, Mr. Inspiration, a dog who had spent in a manner of speaking MORE than a lifetime in the Worthington home, why that was like royalty and a commoner, and it was really going to be tough explaining all this to the national registry, and maybe the real 100 per cent Greyhounds wouldn't be recognized, unless somebody lied through his teeth about the whole thing, and then you'd better hope nobody thought about fawns throwing brindles, and somebody by God was going to pay for all of this, and it was time to hire an attorney, or two, or three, and sue the devil out of Sally and me, for openers, for bringing out a worse than Grade E Greyhound, biggest, dumbest, slowest ox this side of the Mississippi, and next those people who owned the Chinese Chow Chow, and might as well sue the United States Government and the State of Montana for their indiscretionary wolf, by God, and that was for openers, and maybe the thing would end up class action, and abortion, and anti-abortion, and right to life, and right to choice, and some right to life here and the city pound there, and because a dog looked like a wolf, you couldn't tell a book by its cover, and this was by far the worst thing that had ever happened to anybody anywhere any time, and mad hardly covered any of it, at which time Mr. Worthington collapsed, right there in the living room, like a bag of coal, plop and thud, right there on top of his stuffed fawn dog Mr. Inspiration, and I knew Mr. Worthington was as dead as his stuffed dog, Mr. Worthington's eyes matching the one remaining Mr. Inspiration glass eye, and I felt awful, and I knew Sally was upset, I could tell, because she fainted on the couch, and the sheriff arrived, and the county coroner came out, then a mortician and a hearse arrived, and almost tried to haul off Sally, but I said, "No, no not her, she's alive. That's the dead one there," and I pointed to Mr. Worthington on top of Mr. Inspiration, and then questions from the sheriff, and a couple of deputies, and a couple of highway patrol fellows dropped by for a few more questions, maybe to be sociable, I don't know, and Mr. Worthington made his last trip past his maggoty WORTHINGTON mailbox, which arose to the occasion magnificently into a great black swarming tribute, and everybody drove off leaving Sally, Jones and me in the living room with Mr. Inspiration. I looked around, fixed my waking wife a glass of water, then said: "Shall we go?"

Jones yawned, stretched, stood up at the ready, wagged his tail.

Sally nodded and stood up from the couch. I steadied her by the arm.

We filed out the house, down the walk, fanned away at the buzzing flies at the WORTHINGTON mailbox, climbed in the truck and drove for home. Jones sat between us, staring absently down the road.

"The best laid plans of dogs and men often go flat bonkers," I muttered.

"That's familiar," Sally said. "Who said that?"

"McDermutt," I said. "Maddog McDermutt."

EIGHT

Old man Worthington was buried on a Saturday afternoon, in the Ulm nondenominational cemetery, Methodist minister Arnold Swiethzer presiding. Everything took place at the cemetery; there had been no church service. I thought it was a nice ceremony, although lightly attended, but the boys at the track, the ones who had run the Great Falls Track, and a few names I didn't recognize, or hadn't met, had sent flowers and cards, which I found thoughtful. I had read the card, signed by Maddog McDermutt, Ben Dover, Little Elsie, Hugh Mungas, Dogbreath Smith, Fleas Finnegan, Mangy Martinez, Pooch the Mooch McGill. Another wreath of flowers came from Fard's schoolmates. Another I noticed was from the Ulm Does, a female offshoot of the Elk's club, and so I presumed Mr. Worthington at one time or another had been a member of the Elks.

We had sent flowers ourselves, a modest but pretty display which sat next to the dog trainers' wreath. I never said anything when Sally signed it: *Ryan, Sally, and Jones.* I was of the impression Jones, whom we had left home, had better not sign anything, or he was liable to find himself in court. Or tarred and feathered. Or lynched. I was not totally comfortable with the idea Jones had been responsible for the chain of events which led to the untimely demise of Mr.

99

Worthington. In my mind's eye, and I had to agree with Sally, keeping a stuffed dog in the living room, pointed to the television so that it would not be bored, was, indeed, not a normal household phenomenon. Furthermore, Jones certainly was not the father of the wolf or the chow chows.

Mrs. Worthington and Fard sat on folding chairs next to the pit over which the casket of Mr. Worthington teetered. It was my impression Mrs. Worthington was well-oiled for the occasion. At the conclusion of the minister's kind words, Mrs. Worthington let out an awful wail, and it startled me; she burst out sobbing, then quit as sudden as she started, up out of the chair and marched off. The minister shook a few hands, then followed her. I met Fard beside a tall headstone. "Do you have time to drop by and see the litter?" Fard asked.

I leaned on the headstone, glanced at Sally. "I bet they're doing really fine, Fard."

"They are healthy, aggressive pups," Fard said.

"All hale and hearty?" I asked.

"Oh you bet. Everybody. Wolf. Two chow chows. Five Greyhounds. A wonderful, healthy, aggressive litter. I am really sorry Father won't be able to watch them grow up."

"Well, you never know, Fard. He may be watching, you know, from somewhere else. Another dimension, as it were."

"That's true, Mr. McNulty. You're absolutely correct. I have to believe that. I repeat. Can you drop out and see the pups?"

"Sure," I said. "Why not. Twenty minutes?"

"See you there," Fard said.

We pulled up alongside the WORTHINGTON mailbox which did not disappoint us: a black, buzzing cloud rose magnificently as Sally stepped out her side of the truck. Fard hollered from the barn, and we waved, walked over. Inside, Miss Neopolitan was nursing her family. Nothing shy about this litter. The two chow chows dug in and pushed, the Greyhounds pushed back, and the wolf crawled blindly over them all, pushing and shoving, his little fuzzy tail stuck straight up. The Greyhounds all lined up pretty as a picture, tails wagging back and forth, their front paws digging away at Mom.

"Aren't they beauties?" Fard said.

"I'll say," I said, pulling the wolf puppy off a teat. He had a good hold, made a popping noise as I pulled him loose. I looked him over. He squealed. "You don't look so tough," I said. "Who's ascairt of the big bad wolf, eh?" I returned the wolf to the faucet, and he aggressively went at it, as if he had been away for hours. It was hard to believe they were only a few days old.

Sally was looking a chow chow over. "Look at his tail. It's bushy. A Greyhound with a bushy tail. Kind of novel, if you ask me." She put the pup back with the others.

"They really are a fine litter, Fard," I said. "Topnotch, all the way around."

Fard nodded. He seemed depressed, only natural on the day of his father's funeral, and I felt bad about that. It was none of my business, and I shouldn't have asked, but I did anyway: "Where'd your mother go, Fard?"

"I think she went downtown to drown," Fard said, scratching Miss Neopolitan's ear.

"Drowning one's sorrows in a time of grief is somehow to be expected," I said.

"I said drown," Fard said. "It has nothing to do with sorrow. She'll come home mule-faced in a few hours and pass out on the couch."

I glanced at Sally. Long as I was into it, I forged on. "Fard," I said, "are you all right out here? I mean are you attending school all right? You have clothes to wear? Are you eating three meals a day? I don't mean to pry."

"Oh sure," Fard said. "I'm not worried about me. My parents have been alcoholics ever since I can remember. I'm used to that. But I am worried about the pups. I have a fear I won't be able to register them. No registration. No race track. At least for the five Greyhounds."

"Is there something else these pups could do?" Sally asked. "I mean, besides run a race track."

"What else does a racing Greyhound do....but race?" Fard asked.

"Chase coyotes for bounty?" I suggested.

"Maybe," Fard said. "I thought about that. You'd have to find the right person in the right place at the right time. Right now, I don't know who that would be. There aren't any coyotes around here, to speak of."

"How about finding homes for them?" Sally asked. "Look at these pups. They would make wonderful pets, wouldn't they?"

Fard scratched his chin. "I think it'd be tough. The pound in Great Falls put to sleep over a thousand dogs last year nobody wanted."

I looked at Miss Neopolitan mothering her pups. She did not make distinctions between the wolf, the chow chows, the Greyhounds. They were all equal to her and deserved equal love. She would kill for them. She would die for them.

"Fard," I said, holding out my hand for a handshake, man to man. "Keep in touch. You keep those pups healthy. They look great." I leaned over to scratch Miss Neopolitan behind

102

the ear. "And you too, lady. Keep up the good work."

"Thank you, Mr. and Mrs. McNulty, for all that you've done."

I swallowed hard. "You're welcome, Fard. More than welcome. If there is anything more we can do, please let us know."

"I'll do that," Fard said.

"Seriously, Fard," Sally said. "If there is anything, please give us a call."

We climbed in the truck. Fard stood at my window. "I shall do that. I am not shy."

We waved, drove up the road to the bypass, on to the freeway.

Several miles passed before Sally said, "What's that sixth grader going to do with a worthless mixed litter of pups and an alcoholic mother?"

"I don't know," I said. "I'm worried about it, that's for sure."

Another mile passed, and I said, "What about putting a social worker on it, like anonymously phoning in, reporting the situation, maybe he could receive some help that way."

"Child abuse?" Sally said. "Maybe. But what happens then with the litter?"

"Good point," I said. "One way ticket to the pound. Well, for Fard's sake, maybe that's the way it has to go down."

"People survive conditions worse than that," Sally said. "So do animals."

"They're going to need a lot of luck," I said. "Whatever happens, whatever goes down, they're going to have to be lucky."

NINE

I pulled up a chair in the faculty room.

Harry and Sheldon were already in attendance. Harry was seated, sipping away on a coffee cup. Sheldon was in the corner straddling a base fiddle. I dropped my stack of books and papers, headed for the battery acid. To Sheldon, I said, "What now?"

"Oh, I have to restring this thing. The kid put the wrong strings on." He picked up a bow off the counter, took a whack at the beast. The sound that came forth made my teeth itch.

"I see what you mean," I said. "Is that why that thing is called vile?"

"You're late," Harry said, checking his wristwatch against the clock on the wall.

I sat down. "I had a kid didn't understand pronouns."

"That's easy," Sheldon said, cranking down on a squeaky peg. "Pronouns are not amateur nouns."

"That's good," I said. "I'll remember that one."

The principal came in, poured himself a cup, seated him

self, pulled the ashtray over, lit up, and sat there in a cloud of smoke. Between puffs, he looked me over. "Keeping up with your lesson plans, Pardner?" he asked.

"I try to," I said.

"Good good good," he said. "Keep up the good work."

Harry said, "I read in the paper a fellow Greyhound aficionado bit the dust this weekend."

Sheldon said, "Quite an obituary. Said the man, what was his name?"

"Worthington," I said.

"Worthington." Sheldon was stuffing a wire string into the waste basket. "Paper said he had had quite a career in Greyhound racing. Listed a whole bunch of famous dogs."

Dr. Mayonaisse, who never participated in our conversations, asked. "Did you know the man?"

"Yes," I said. "I did. Yes."

"What'd he die of?" Harry wanted to know.

I thought about it. "Heart attack probably. Liver. Kidneys. Stroke. All of the above. I don't know. The guy blew up."

"You were there?" Sheldon said. He had the base fiddle on its back, and he straddled it like he was going to ride it out the door. "You saw the guy croak?"

"I was there," I said. I felt funny, wondered if I wasn't getting high on Dr. Mayonaisse's cigarette smoke.

"Guy just dropped, huh?" Harry said.

"I was just a couple of blocks away at the time," Sheldon said. "Just down the road. I have a friend out there with an Irish setter, wanted to breed to Bobo the Great, but she wasn't ready yet. The guy paid me $500 stud fee, plus pick of the litter, just to make sure Bobo would be the father. Little extra cash never hurt anybody. I did see the ambulance and sheriff and highway patrol drive by."

Harry said, "I had a guy call me, wanted to breed his black lab to Montana Black Satan. Maybe in about a month. Monty gets $500 for his services also. How about you, McNulty, how's that dog of yours coming along?"

"Jones? He's.......... fine, thanks."

Harry laughed. "What's Jones' stud fee?"

Sheldon over in the corner giggled.

I had the feeling I was in for a rough prep period.

The counselor, I still didn't know her name, came in to save my bacon. She read from a pass that apparently Sheldon had written. Sheldon had one foot on the base fiddle, still on its back, and was trying to thread a string. He wasn't quite long enough to reach the string on the nut and turn the peg. I got up, went over to help, put my thumb on the string to put pressure on the nut. "Thanks," Sheldon said, moving down to the peg. "Can you hold the bridge up with your other hand?" Then, to the counselor, he said, "I'm sorry. Could you repeat that?"

The counselor read again.

"Dick Strickford. Orchestra 1. Fifth Period. Discipline Request. *Dick continues to eat his sheet music throughout the period.* How can we best help this student? *Perform a frontal lobotomy?* Mr. Adamson, I find that very unprofessional."

Harry burst out laughing. I had to laugh. Sheldon nodded, grinned, cranked away on his peg. Dr. Mayonaisse turned.

He looked at the base fiddle. "What's that?" He asked.

"It's a violin for a very big kid," Harry said.

I really anticipated that Harry had crossed the line on that one. I would never have talked to my boss like that.

Dr. Mayonaisse was on the rise. He snuffed out his cigarette, said, "Hello there" to the counselor on his way by, paused at the door, and said, "I'll pass that information along to the football coach. Whoever that kid is, he'd make a wonderful tackle. Have a good day. Keep those lesson plans coming."

The counselor followed the principal.

"What is that woman's name?" I said.

"I have no idea," Harry said, refilling his cup with battery acid.

"Who cares," Sheldon said. "Grab that big fat string off the counter there, will you?"

TEN

I was busy going over a writing assignment, not too happy. Either I could not teach much, or I had a class of dunderheads. My students were not catching on. I was sick of reading papers. Jones sat under the table, his head on my knee. I scratched his ear with one hand as I marked up Billy Watson's paper with a red pencil with the other hand. Near as I could tell Billy Watson made no sense whatsoever. And I didn't know how to help him. Billy's paper started badly, then went thick. I could not see what one word had to do with any other word. I started over. Maybe I missed something. Jones turned his head so that I could scratch the other ear. My wife yelled from the kitchen:

"Maddog McDermutt calling! Collect!"

What a nice break from my papers. I picked up the phone. "Hello Mr. McDermutt. Nice to hear from you."

Mr. McDermutt suggested it would be wonderful if I could help him over the Christmas break, spend a week with his racing Greyhound kennel, help him break down the kennel for his next booking, Yuma, Arizona. He would drive to Yuma; I would fly home to Great Falls, around the First of January, in plenty of time to teach school.

"It'd be a nice break from teaching," McDermutt said. "You could see how the other half lives."

I had to agree with him there. I put my hand over the mouthpiece and hissed to my wife, who was leaning against the wall, listening in curiously. "Maddog McDermutt has invited me to help him run his kennel at Key West, Florida, over the Christmas break."

Sally did not seem overly enthused. She shrugged.

Coincidentally, it so happened my wife was going to be tied up for the Christmas vacation with her mother, who had been scheduled for minor surgery and had made a special request her daughter be nearby throughout. "It was," I told Mr. McDermutt, "a possibility."

Jones walked in the kitchen for a drink of water.

"What about Jones?" Sally asked.

"Could I bring Jones?" I asked.

"Of course," Maddog said. "In time. In time. But not this booking. We are having problems here, and Jones is better off in Montana at this time."

"Sally has to go out of town, Maddog. I don't want to put him in the pound or a kennel. Besides, I want to see him run."

"Take Jones out to my godson, little Fardington Maddog Worthington, and Jones can have the run of the place out there. He'll love it. Fard will take good care of ol' Jones. What do you say?"

I said, "No thanks. No Jones. No McNulty."

112

Perhaps it was something I had to do. If I had to work it out of my system, better now than later. Going to the dogs for a vacation would do me good, change my attitudes forever, maybe help me grow a little, see how the other half lives. Teaching school seemed isolated, protected, not in touch with the real world. Who knows what I would learn about life, about my fellow man, about animals, about what makes the world go around. What wealth of experiences would I eventually bring from Key West to my English classes?

And so I bought a shipping crate, watched Jones get loaded into the baggage compartment, then I boarded the Frontier airliner, for Florida, via Denver, then Atlanta. Jones and I rode an Eastern puddle-jumper to Key West where we were met by Little Elsie, Hugh Mungas, Mangy Martinez, Dogbreath Smith, Ben Dover, Pooch the Mooch McGill, Fleas Finnegan, and the big guy, the man in the pink jump suit, Maddog McDermutt, who rushed up to the gate and stuck his big paw over, shook my hand, a big grin across his physiognomy, and said, "Welcome to Key West!" And around the group I went with re-introductions. "Hello," I said. "Nice to see you again." "How are you." And I could not help but notice, they all seemed like nice people, mind you, but they continually were digging at themselves, Pooch the Mooch McGill bending over to scratch his ankle, Maddog tipping back his Stetson hat to dig at his head, Fleas and Mangy scratching away at their belly buttons, which I thought maybe a little tacky, and I had to wonder what we had going on here.

A baggage cart rattled along, and I waved the driver over. To his annoyance, and to the astonishment of the dog trainers, I opened the shipping crate door and Jones jumped down.

Maddog gasped. "You don't turn Greyhounds loose like that!"

"Jones?" I said. "Jones doesn't need a leash."

Jones took a long, deep stretch, like he was taking a bow, his butt up in the air, sighed, scratched his nails on the tarmac, yawned, farted, then trotted along the fence to a palm tree which he saluted.

Maddog and Fleas set Jones' shipping crate in the back of Maddog's pickup truck. I picked up my suitcase, tossed it in back, opened the door for Jones, Jones jumped in, and we all went for a late lunch.

Jones remained in the truck, at Maddog's suggestion.

"He's an English professor," Maddog said, winking at Fleas Finnegan, who scratched and tugged at his crotch before he sat down.

"I teach junior high ninth grade," I said. "I'm a teacher, not a professor."

"Around this bunch, you're a professor," Maddog said, and everybody laughed. I felt very relaxed. Seemed like a great collection of people. As my dad would have said, "The salt of the earth." And I responded by buying lunch, mainly because the ticket had found its way to the bottom of my plate. But I did not mind. I presumed everybody kept mental track, and in time everybody pitched in, took a turn. That only seemed natural and fair.

"Ol' Jones has put on some weight," Maddog said.

"Indeed he has, Maddog," I said. "I think Jones has become the fastest dog in the world."

And everybody roared. It startled me.

"Did I say something humorous?" I asked.

"Relax," Maddog said, patting me on the knee. "This crew was in Great Falls, you know, and they remember that big dog lumbering on to the first turn and forgetting to turn and running in to the fence."

And everybody laughed again.

"He does not run in to fences now," I said. "You haven't seen Jones run lately. He's a new dog, and he will suck the hair off any dog you have at this track."

And they laughed again. Oh, my goodness, did they laugh.

"OK, Ryan, don't take it serious. We laugh at a lot of things. I'm sure ol' Jones has really improved. How much does he weigh did you say?"

"102 pounds," I said.

Oh the trainers thought that was humorous; they slapped the table, and the glasses and plates bounced up and down, and tears ran down their cheeks, and they roared and elbowed each other and pointed at me.

I glanced outside. Jones sat on the front seat of the pickup, panting, waiting.

"He's not one Greyhound; he's two Greyhounds," Fleas Finnegan said, and I thought a couple of them were going to be sick, laughing so hard.

When the frivolity of the moment lingered, I threw in my two bits. "I presume Maddog told you part of the deal was that I would be able to race Jones."

The trainers stared at me. Then it started again, a guffaw here, a grunt there; somebody slobbered down his face across the table, and around they went again like idiots recently re-leased from the local asylum to pass judgment on the latest Three Stooges movie, and while they were at it they scratched their belly buttons, their heads, their crotches, their legs.

I leaned over and asked Maddog: "What is the matter with them?"

He patted me on the knee. "Nothing. We're having lunch."

And on that everybody arose, like the minister had announced Hymn 100, grab your book and sing, buster; now they all had to go somewhere, the bathroom the way they were acting, and I picked up the bill, paid it, and it was considerable, and I might add nobody said thanks, and I found myself climbing into Maddog McDermutt's truck, patting Jones on the head, and off to the track we went, down the highway, down the off-road, and I could see the track, the tote sticking up, the fence trying to stand straight, the grandstands, and we drove through the security gate, waved at the security guard, and stopped in front of Maddog's kennel.

I set my suitcase down, followed Maddog in, looked at the crates.

"Where does Jones go?" I asked.

"What?" Maddog said.

"Jones. He's still in the truck. Where does Jones go?"

"Why don't you put him in the turnout pen. Then we'll make up a bed for him down on the end, on the bottom."

I went for the truck, opened the door, and Jones jumped down. "Hey!" The Security Guard hollered. "Put a leash on that dog!"

"He's all right," I said.

Jones followed me inside, touched noses with all the dogs on the bottom as he moved through the kennel to the turnout pen. He gave me that look I had come to know so well, like *what are we doing here, stupid?*

All of Maddog's dogs seemed restless. About half of them had their butts to the wire, rubbing back and forth. You could hear others sniffing, biting, licking, teeth clicking. "Hi there," I said to a little fawn bitch whom I interrupted digging at her tail. She looked up at me and seemed to nod back. "Pretty dog," I said to Maddog.

"Lovely little lady," Maddog agreed. He was pouring water out the end of a hose into a big porcelain tub. He then added something, a powdery substance, to the water. It stunk. A chemical smell, sulfur maybe, something else too, like burnt gas. Ammonia too was coming to mind. "What is that?" I asked.

"My own formula," Maddog said, scratching his left armpit. "We have a flea problem down here."

"Oh?" I said. My pits had itched ever since I had walked in to the kennel; now I knew why. Watching Maddog scratch his armpit made it worse, and as tacky as it might seem, I scratched my armpit too.

"Isn't the bubonic plague, the black death that wiped out half of Europe on several occasions, carried by fleas off wharf rats?" I asked.

"These are racing Greyhounds, not wharf rats," Maddog said. "Here. Watch." He helped a black dog jump out a crate, and by the collar led him to the tub, lifted the dog, dropped him in the solution, then said to me, "Put those rubber gloves on and get over here."

I put on the pair of gloves; and I got over there.

Maddog said: "You want to make sure you kill these rotten buggers. Fleas like it behind the ears, under the tail around the bunghole. There goes one!" And yes I could see it, no, not it, them, two, three, four, poor dog, little black fleas heading for the cover of the longer hairs on the leg, then another took a run for it. "They like it around the eyes, too. Eyes, butt, anywhere damp. Take this sponge and dab around that bunghole area, yes, like that, then around the ears, right, dab around the eyes, right, then grab that bucket there, and soak the whole dog, squeeze the sponge, atta boy, you are going to be a great dog trainer, and I am going to take a nap. I will see you in three hours for turnouts, feeding, schooling races, then we'll catch something to eat, then the races, then we'll feed the schoolers and racers, last turnout, then we'll go catch a snack."

"Sounds like a full day," I said, and Maddog was out the door.

I finished the black dog. Now what? I lifted him out of the tub, and he promptly shook himself, and I was wet from Maddog's concoction. Maddog McDermutt's pink jump suit was making sense. "Thanks," I said to the dog. The sopped dog looked back at me. I pulled his muzzle off, then dipped it in the solution. Might as well be complete, I thought. Then I looked at the muzzle, then the dog. Something didn't look right. Greenhorn Ryan suddenly realized he did not know how to put the muzzle on. Jones never wore one. Like that? I pushed. The dog looked at me like I wasn't very bright. I turned the thing upside down. It still did not go. Finally, after a little trial and error, I learned how to put on a racing Greyhound's wire muzzle. "Thanks," I said to the black dog, "for your patience." I led the dog outside. Jones, lying down in a corner, watched. The black dog squatted and P-d, then stared at me, stared at Jones, then went over to the corner of the yard, turned around and around, then lay down to lick himself. I found that odd. The black dog was a male dog. Ol' Jones now, he would have lifted his leg. Maybe that was learned behavior, I couldn't say. It didn't matter, I was busting. There did not seem to be any restroom nearby; I stepped to an adjacent corner, looked up and down the rows of kennels to make sure I was unobserved, and took a leak myself. "What are you looking at?" I said to the black dog. Jones stood up, sniffed, lifted his leg to compliment my statement. The black dog squatted, made it unanimous.

I went inside the kennel and counted dogs. Forty-five, one in the yard. I was going to dip all these dogs, one at a time, in a tub of gunk that only came up to the dogs' knees? In three hours? No way. Greyhound trainers operated like this? The technique was out of the dark ages. And I was out the door on the hunt for a bigger container. Liquids, water mainly, was my specialty, ex all-American swimmer that I was, and volume here was a problem. I was a school teacher. I would be creative. I wandered all over the compounds and found nothing suitable. You needed something deeper.....like a cattle watering trough. Well, this was Florida, not Montana. I smelled the ocean air. I took a deep breath. It was great. Absolutely great. A tub of water big enough? Salt?

Salt will kill anything. Well, McNulty, do you think the Atlantic Ocean big enough? Well? Well! Don't poison them, or yourself. Drown 'em.

And I was back into the kennel, and I leashed up ten dogs, five for each hand, and I was out the door, "Come on, Jones," the dogs pulling and striking out ahead, and past the startled security gate guard, who said, "Hey! Where you going with them dogs? That one dog is off his lead again!"

"He's OK. Just a little exercise," I said. "My name is Ryan McNulty. I'm Maddog McDermutt's new assistant trainer. That's my own dog, Down Under Jones."

"Right," he said. "Maddog mentioned you'd be here for the afternoon. Glad to know you. Watch out for snakes."

"Oh we'll stick to the roads. Where's the nearest water? I haven't seen the ocean in years."

He pointed. "Right over there, not very far. Follow the path."

"Right," I said. "Thanks. Come on, Jones."

And off we marched, the dogs enthusiastically into it, pulling, and soon we were at something that resembled a beach, and I waded in, and the dogs hesitated, testing the water with their tongues, making faces at the salt taste, then they waded in; they stood there, enjoying the water, standing on their tippy-toes, heads above the water line.

"You coming, Jones?"

Jones waded in up to his belly button.

I watched the dogs closely to see if any fleas would make a swim for it. Nothing yet. I put all ten leashes in my left hand, and splashed water on the ears, turning the dog's head to dip the entire ear, then the other ear, holding it down as long as the dog would tolerate it, then they'd flop their ears and everybody blinked from the sting of the salt water in their eyes. Some of the dogs started to swim a little at the end of their leads, not much, floating up and down with the waves, keeping in touch with the bottom with their nails. Jones went swimming by, circled back. I hoped this worked because it sure beat that stupid tub Maddog McDermutt had. I wondered how my wife was doing with her mother; if she could only see me now. I wondered what my English students back in Great Falls would think if they could see their teacher up to his keester in the Atlantic Ocean with ten racing Greyhounds. This was not Ivanhoe or Romeo and Juliet. This was real. This was where it was. I couldn't believe how well-behaved the dogs were, how gentle, how gracious, how patient. They were really neat dogs. I must have been the luckiest man on earth. Maybe I had died and gone to heaven. I became aware my crotch did not itch any more, but my belly button did. The little buggers were moving to higher ground. The weather was wonderfully warm; I waded on in, up to my armpits, and the racers all performed a natural dog paddle at the end of their leashes. Jones returned to the sandy beach, where he rolled in a pile of kelp.

I lifted a dog's tail to see if I could see fleas. I dug around a little, and yes, a flea, and it swam off. So fleas can swim. You learn something every day.

"I think they're running out of air," I said to Jones. He stood up, kelp draped over his shoulder, then sat to watch.

We stayed there for some time. If you are going to drown

a flea, I thought, might as well drown it right. I checked my wristwatch. Give it a half hour, I thought. Very scientific. Later, I would find a glass of salt water, pick a flea off a dog, and see exactly how long it took to drown the little creep. Or kill it with salt water. Either way was better than that stupid tub.

We waded out of the Atlantic, returned to the kennel, Jones leading the way past the Security Guard, and I leashed up ten more and repeated this routine until I was finished. Everybody in the kennel had had a bath. Jones had had five baths and five rolls in kelp. Nobody was scratching. Everybody, including Jones, was nestled in the paper beds, snoozing comfortably.

Maddog was back.

"Finished?" he said.

"Yup," I said.

He looked at the tub. "How come so much is left?"

I shrugged.

He looked in the crates at the dogs.

"Nobody's scratching," he said, then added, "Tomorrow we'll disinfect the crates, and the entire kennel, turnout yard too."

I hadn't thought of that. Of course. Fleas would have laid eggs everywhere. You'd have to kill them, too. I wondered where I could find a hose long enough and a pump, maybe a diesel air compressor for a pump, so that I could spray this place with sea water. There must be another way. Maddog's technique of disinfecting his kennel was to probably put the dogs out in the yard, then go around the kennel with a hammer, killing fleas one at a time. Maybe we could take the kennel to the ocean. I would think on it.

"Time to feed," Maddog said.

And we fed the dogs, but not the racers and schoolers.

Then we took the racers to the track.

Then we schooled pups.

Then we brought the schoolers back to the kennel.

Then we fed the schoolers.

Then we had a hot-dog I wouldn't feed the dogs. I paid for my own, no more.

The soft drinks weren't too bad.

Even though I bought soft drinks all around, it did hit the spot.

Then we watched twelve races.

Then we turned all the Greyhounds out again.

Then we fed the racers.

Then we went for a snack.

"Does anybody ever go to bed around here?" I asked.

"You have to take a nap," Hugh Mungas said, "if you want to make it through the day."

"I seemed to have missed my nap today," I said.

Maddog cleared up the matter. "Ryan here spent the afternoon dipping for fleas."

Everybody nodded. I was surprised. I thought they'd burst out laughing on that one, on principal.

"What'd you use?" Little Elsie wanted to know.

"Something short of pure creosote, the usual," Maddog said.

"Did it work?" Pooch the Mooch wanted to know. "I think

around here fleas drink creosote as an appetizer."

"Seemed to work," Maddog said. "I didn't see any fleas on the racers or schoolers."

"My dogs are going to scratch their hides plum off," Ben Dover said. "The only way I can kill the little buggers is to pick them off the dog, one at a time, and squash 'em."

I guess I was not far off my McDermutt / hammer theory.

"What concentration did you use?" Hugh wanted to know.

"Strong as I could without burning the hide off the dog," Maddog said.

"Maddog," I said, "I have a confession to make. I didn't dip your dogs in the tub."

It grew silent around the table; everybody was staring at me.

"You didn't?" Maddog finally said.

"No. I took the dogs all down to the ocean and drowned the fleas."

Maddog sounded like an echo. "You took them all down to the ocean and drowned 'em?"

"Yessir."

Maddog cleared his sinuses.

Fleas Finnegan down at the other end of the table blew bubbles in his coke through a straw.

Then Maddog laughed. He slapped the table. He put his arm around me and gave me a hug and kissed me on the neck. Then everybody was laughing. You never heard such a ruckus. Finally, Ben Dover said, "I never heard of anything so stupid."

And everybody roared.

They slapped the table, they pointed at me, tears rolled down their cheeks, and they could not stop. They went on for ten minutes like that, elbowing each other, and one would try to speak, but couldn't, and it went on and on something awful.

Finally Maddog put his arm around me and led me out the door, everybody following, holding their sides from laughing so hard, and I piled in Maddog's truck, and he drove on home, a house trailer on its last leg, and he showed me my bed, if that's what you could call it, and I never bothered to put on my pajamas; I collapsed and passed out immediately.

What must have been four hours later Maddog was shaking me out of bed. I did not have to dress. I also did not shave, wash, or go potty. What I did was climb back in the truck and sit zombie fashion on the passenger side as Maddog drove for the kennels.

"Weren't we just here?" I asked, and my throat was full of stuff, my voice raspy. I hoped I wasn't sick.

Maddog rolled down his window and waved at seven men and one woman standing crotch deep in the Atlantic Ocean. Even with their hands full of dog leashes, they still attempted to wave back.

"Come on," Maddog said. "I want to show you how to thaw out the meat, and how to feed 'em properly. Then we'll disinfect the kennels."

"You know, Maddog," I said, "yesterday when we turned in the racers to the paddocks......"

"Jinny pit," Maddog said. "Horses it's paddocks. Dogs it's jinny pit."

"Right," I said. "Jinny pit. Well let's presume I killed all the fleas on your dogs, OK?"

Maddog pulled up in front of his kennel door, and killed the engine. He looked at me. "That'd be awesome."

"And let's say we kill all the fleas in the crates, in the cracks, in the paper, out in the yard, fumigate the joint, I mean nothing short of mass murder."

"Right," Maddog said.

"Well yesterday you turned in your racers to the jinny pit and so did everybody else and why can't they pick up fleas in there?"

Maddog nodded. "That's always a problem," he said.

"Well we better fumigate that place while we're at it," I said.

"Lots of luck on that one," Maddog said.

Hugh and Little Elsie were walking by with ten Greyhounds apiece, back from an ocean dip.

Maddog looked at me. "It's a great idea," he said. "Let's set the meat to thaw. I have another little job for your consideration."

And we piled out of the truck.

We turned the dogs out in the turnout yard, and, as instructed, I went around the yard with my shovel, and I filled two buckets with you know what.

"That's right. Quick before another dog steps in it."

And we set the meat to thaw.

And Maddog showed me his feeding formula, and warned me not to tell any of the others. "My secret," Maddog said.

Then we went for breakfast.

Then I phoned a couple of commercial pest companies for a couple of bids on fumigating the entire place for fleas.

Then I returned to the table to pick up the tab.

Then we drove back to the track.

It was coming to me these dog trainers were not human. It was not possible to keep going, day after day, with the hours these people put in. I had been on the job not a full twenty-four hours yet, and school teaching was beginning to look pretty good, although, I must add, it did not have the charm. Would I rather work with dogs or kids? At this moment it was a tossup. Hard to tell. Give me a day or two.

One of the kids in one of my classes, when we were doing Ivanhoe (was that only two months ago?), asked: "Well where did all the knights in shining armor go?"

Clever teacher that I was, I creatively answered: "They all became cowboys."

"Well where'd they go?"

"They became truck drivers."

Now I knew that was the wrong answer.

They became dog trainers.

I found a phone and called Sally.

"Has Jones run yet?" she wanted to know.

ELEVEN

"I minored in drama in college, you know," Maddog said from time to time. He said it at railside; he said it at weigh-in; he said it in the compounds; he said it in the clubhouse; he said it at the sprint paths; he said it at the coffee house; he said it at schooling races. He had said it all so many times in the last two days, reminiscent of the little boy who always cried wolf because he was lonesome, and everybody came running, until finally everybody wised up, and nobody came, and this time there really was a wolf, and the wolf ate the kid, and maybe I missed the point of the story, but I personally was rooting for the wolf all along. I never did care much for that kid. So when Maddog mentioned that he had minored in drama in college, we had all heard it so many times, Maddog received responses like:

"Oh."

"Yeah."

"Right."

"Uh..huh."

Sometimes when a dull and boring race transpired, Maddog would lecture us and say his favorite dramatic genre was not tragedy, or high comedy as anybody who knew his finer talents might suspect, and it wasn't melodrama either, but it was farce, true farce, or theater of the absurd, and his favorite play was an Ionesco, a play about idiots, performed for idiots, and on that everybody bought subscriptions, eagerly, nodding heads in total agreement.

At the end of one race, Pooch the Mooch McGill jumped on Maddog good when he asked Maddog: "You ever hear of type casting?"

"Boys. Boys. Boys," Maddog said, his great baritone booming, "Christmas is upon us and I have had an idea."

Moans and groans all around. Maddog put one arm up on the fence and adjusted his granny glasses with the other. He tilted his dirty white Stetson up, adjusted his love beads.

"Maddog," Fleas said, "when are you going to wash that filthy pink jump suit?" Fleas reached out and tried to flick a crumb off Maddog's mustard-stained pink jump suit, but it wouldn't flick, then Fleas tried to scrape it off with his fingernail, and it wouldn't scrape, then Fleas tried to grab it between his thumb and forefinger, and he squeezed and pulled, but whatever it was would not budge. I wished Fleas hadn't done that, because since I had arrived here in Key West I had made it a point to ignore it. It was too big to be a goober. Maddog brushed Fleas' hand away and tweaked his VOTE REPUBLICAN button, straightening it just a touch.

What a specimen, I thought. The mold broke when they made this guy.

Maddog again: "I have been doing a little PR work with management, being as Christmas is just around the corner. So listen up."

Little Elsie walked out of the crowd to join us. "What's happening, guys?"

"We're gonna do a little PR work," Fleas said. "The Scot with the short deck syndrome has had an idea."

"No thanks," Little Elsie said, turning to leave, but Fleas grabbed her arm.

"I have written a play," Maddog said.

"I thought you were an actor," Ben Dover said.

"Many actors return to the pen," Maddog said, talking to us like we were children. "Shakespeare, you know, was an actor."

"I refuse to be in a Christmas play," Ben Dover said. "I played one of the three kings in Sunday School, and my good friend Tommy who was playing a shepherd tripped and about tore my head off with his shepherd's crook and everybody in the whole church thought that was very funny. I was embarrassed. I had a red ring around my neck for two months like somebody had tried to hang me, and I won't have any of it."

"I remember in Sunday School I stood around the barn in the nativity scene," Hugh Mungas said. "I think I was a cow or a horse or something."

"I played one of the three kings," Fleas said proudly. "Done a good job, too. No shepherd hooked me with his crook. You have a bad attitude, Ben Dover."

"I was a camel in the first grade," Pooch the Mooch McGill said.

"I was an angel," Little Elsie said.

"You still are," Fleas Finnegan said.

I was trying to remember where and when the angel came in when Maddog said: "You're on the wrong track again. We're going to do Santa Claus this year; I have had an idea you won't believe."

"Oh I believe that I won't believe your idea, Maddog," Fleas said.

"Well?" Pooch the Mooch McGill said, "What is it?"

Maddog took a deep breath. Here it comes, I thought. For some reason I thought of Dr. Mayonaisse. "Well, we all have a dog that is laid off and isn't doing anything anyway. Right?"

Everybody nodded. Sure did.

"Like a big dog. A strong dog. A big chesty dog. An aggressive dog. A dog that stands tall and proud."

Everybody nodded. I thought of Jones. Maddog, upon my growing impatience, stuck to his story that Jones' papers were on the way. Jones could not step foot on the track without papers. I was not pleased.

Maddog continued: "A dog that could impersonate a reindeer."

A reindeer? I ran a reindeer around in my head. Nothing happened in the gray matter. Try the other part. No. Nothing there either.

I said, "Did you say reindeer, Maddog?"

"You bet," Maddog said, into it now. "Boys, the McDermutt Kennel will donate Down Under Jones," and when he said it, I have to admit I was a little bit thrilled. "And Little Elsie, what do you have?"

"Well now wait one minute, Maddog," Little Elsie said. "What are we doing with these dogs? What do you want these dogs turned reindeer for?"

"I found a dog sled."

Pooch the Mooch summed it up: "In Key West, Florida?"

"It was on sale. I couldn't pass it up. Well, don't you boys understand?" Maddog demanded.

"No!" we chorused.

"I'm going to play Santa," Maddog said. I noticed his voice changed, and filled with something. Humility maybe. Modesty? He went on: "You boys and Little Elsie can be my elves!"

Nobody moved. Nobody said anything.

"Management," Maddog said, "was extremely enthusiastic. The situation is go. We're on. There's no stopping now. The show must go on."

"Pooch, I am going to appoint you and Fleas the antler men. I want you to dig up some screen wire, mold it, find some flour and paste, remember like you did in grade school, and make some antlers. Mix them up, you know, a royal here, a monarch there, a pride there, nice group of antlers."

"Dibs on the monarch," Mangy Martinez said.

"My dog wants to be the lead dog," Hugh Mungas said.

"Then what?" I asked, wishing that I hadn't, but somebody had to ask.

"Then we take little cords and tie the antlers to the dogs' muzzle straps. You guys catchin' on?"

"I've never had any drama courses, Maddog," Pooch the Mooch McGill said.

Maddog was on his soapbox now. He continued: "We're going to make a grand entrance." Maddog pointed over to the gate where we met for schooling races, the gate where the tractors and cars drive out onto the track. "Before the Ninth Race, we will enter over there," he said, pointing again, "with eight dogs, Dancer, Prancer, Donner and Blitzen, Dasher, Basher, Hasher, and Masher, are you beginning to see the light, boys? Have I opened the curtain and turned up the lights, and can you see the stage, and you fellows will be dressed up like elves, and I will be dressed up like Santa. And the reindeer, really racing Greyhounds, will pull Santa on his sled down the track, across the finish line, and I'll wave, and you guys can wave too, and we'll all wave, and the fans will all wave back, and it'll be nice, and it'll be Christmasy, and it'll be fun, and I bet we all earn a nice round of applause for our efforts, too."

"How you gonna pull a dog sled?" Ben Dover asked. "The runners will stick in the track sand."

"It has wheels, boy. This dog sled has wheels. The guy who sold it to me trains huskies up north, when he isn't playing tuba for the Salvation Army in Panama City. Then, when he races up in Montana or up in Canada or up in Alaska or up in the Klondike he takes his dogs and sled and takes the wheels off and over the snow they go. He has several sleds and generously sold me this one for a song."

Then Maddog grew serious, confidential. "This sled," Maddog said, "has been in sled dog races."

"Takes all kinds," Pooch the Mooch said. "Can't imagine anybody running along after a bunch of dogs day in and day out in 50 below weather."

Maddog asked: "Well? Are you in?"

"Oh sure, Maddog, gimme five," Fleas said, and everybody slapped hands like Maddog had sunk a fifty footer, with his eyes closed, backwards, and then we shook on it, then we went and bought popcorn, and then we headed for the final turnouts. I thought, as I walked across the dark, why not. Seemed harmless enough. Eight dogs weren't doing anything anyway, give them something to do. Jones, something of a ham, might even enjoy it. And if we could wish somebody a Merry Christmas by dressing up like elves, well then why not. By the time I reached the kennel door, and I could hear the dogs all stirring when they heard me, I felt kind of good about the whole thing. I turned on the light. "Hey dogs," I said. "Guess what?"

The next day Mangy brought rented elf suits by the kennel, and I tried one on, and it didn't fit too well, a little tight around the stomach, too loose in the legs, but sort of pretty, green, with a little robin hood hat, a nice sash belt that tied at the side, green tights, and Mangy said it really was a Robin Hood style more than a north pole fashion, but I said I didn't think anybody would know the difference; it was the spirit of the thing that counted, and Mangy agreed and moved on to see how Pooch The Mooch looked in his.

Then Maddog came by on a noon turnout with a script. Maddog made sure we all realized he had sacrificed several afternoon naps to write it. He gathered us all together, down by the dump, where everybody throws the you-know-what, on the other side of this big pile of you-know-what because

Maddog didn't want anybody to see us rehearsing, and we practiced jumping around some, and yelling, in unison, "Merry Christmas!"

And, "Happy New Year!"

But Maddog had it written that we do that once every fourth time. " Merry Christmas. Merry Christmas. Merry Christmas." One right after the other, then a "Happy New Year," no more, no less, although Pooch the Mooch McGill and Mangy Martinez had trouble with the timing; invariably one of them would jump in too early; then we'd have to stop and start all over; but Maddog had patience and complimented us on our good spirits and how hard we tried, and if we kept working at it, we'd perfect it before too long.

We also practiced waving and smiling, especially the smiling. The jumping around part came kind of natural because of all the flies buzzing around, big horse flies we used to call them back in Montana, I mean big buggers, the kind that flew up out of the WORTHINGTON mailbox, but the smiling came harder. Everybody worked hard on the smiling part, and Maddog became a difficult task master. He said he had not only written the script, somebody had to be the director and block out all the actors, and since he was the only one of the bunch that had any experience in theater he would take that responsibility, and we could all be glad of it, and I think we were, and at first Ben Dover thought Maddog meant we were all blockheads and became sort of testy, but later Ben learned Maddog meant positioning, and everybody thought he could have said so in the first place. I thought about telling Maddog he wasn't the only one who had drama courses in college, but I didn't. Finally, Maddog said everybody had it down pretty good, and asked Pooch and Fleas how the antlers were coming, and Fleas said all they had to do was paint them brown, that they looked pretty darned good, and Mangy said his dog was black, and Ben Dover said his dog was fawn, and Maddog hadn't thought of that and he said, "Well, we have to do one of two things. We have to color the antlers to the colors of the dogs, or we have to color the dogs to the antlers. In that reindeer only come in one color, as writer and director of this production I have decided all the dogs will be of one color."

"What color is that, Maddog?" Fleas asked.

"Reindeer color, of course, to match the antlers."

"Of course," Hugh Mungas said. "As long as my dog goes first."

"I'll bet they ask us to do this next year," Pooch the Mooch McGill said.

"I'm worried, boys," Maddog said, "about it catching on, the other tracks will copy us. They always do copy a good idea, you know, and then we'll get ripped off, and somebody else will get the credit. Those of us who have all the good ideas never get the full credit in the end you know. Seems to be the way of the world."

"Can you copyright or patent something like this?" I asked.

"I don't know," Maddog said, rubbing his chin. "I don't know. I'd sure hate to see somebody rip off this one. This one could go big time. Dog tracks that run through Christmas are going to jump on this idea, and we once again will receive nothing for our troubles. We should receive a small royalty for every performance."

"Well," I said, hoping to smooth matters somewhat, "we could subscribe to Ben Franklin's philosophy that all inventions should be philanthropic. Everyone should share in the benefits and the inventor should not be selfish about it."

"That has merit," Little Elsie said.

"It is Christmas, after all, Maddog McDermutt," Fleas Finnegan said. "We're supposed to be in the spirit of giving, and all you do is worry about somebody stealing your great idea. I think we should not worry about that sort of thing."

"Fine," Maddog mumbled. "Fine." He went off shaking his head.

"Grinch," Fleas grumbled.

Then Maddog turned to announce: "Tomorrow, same time, right here, for a stage rehearsal. I want you boys to be dressed up in costume, with your dogs, forget their makeup, but we'll try the antlers, see if they fit and all, and see how they take to the traces, and then we'll really be ready." Maddog snorted, wiped his nose on his sleeve, and waddled off, his script sticking out the back pocket of his pink jump suit.

The stage rehearsal went all right, I guess. I dressed up in my green Robin Hood suit, put the harness on Jones, and he stood there obviously wondering what was going on now, embarrassed, as dogs do get embarrassed, and the other boys' dogs looked about the same. Who says dogs don't think. This was a new one on them. They were not very enthusiastic about the idea, looked like to me, Jones included. Maddog had taken the time to put little bells on the harness, and they tinkled as the dogs moved.

"What a nice-looking dog sled," Little Elsie said, walking down one side of it, and we all agreed. It did look nice. It had four bicycle wheels, the balloon kind, and axles welded to the rails. Looked sturdy. Maddog stood on a platform mounted on the rails and had taken precautions to offset his weight with eight sacks of dog food loaded in the front of the sled. Obviously, the sled needed the ballast in front, or it would have stood on end when Maddog mounted the back, gone up in the air and hung a few dogs in the process. It was beginning to look like Maddog had thought of everything. It was a good thing he had a script because otherwise I was sure he would have forgotten something. Too many details.

"Don't those little bells add the right touch," Ben Dover said, flicking one with his forefinger, and the bell tinkled merrily away.

"Very Christmasy," Mangy Martinez agreed.

We all agreed. The bells kind of set everything off.

Then Pooch and Ben handed out the antlers, and we snapped them on with bunji cords to the kennel muzzle straps, and you know what, they didn't look bad. If you used your imagination a little, the dogs did look like Santa's reindeer. But this was stage rehearsal; don't jump the gun. So we all patted ourselves on the backs, and talked about how the crowd would love us, and we patted the dogs and congratulated them too, and the dogs caught on a little and perked up and barked here and there, like they enjoyed impersonating reindeer, and so we broke up mighty enthusiastic, wishing each other "Merry Christmas," and I took Jones back to the kennel, took his antlers off, and turned him out a minute in the turnout yard, then put him in his crate and as he bunked down, I wished him a "Merry Christmas," and he thumped his tail in return, and I wished all the dogs in the kennel a "Merry Christmas" before I went to watch the races.

After the Eighth Race we met Maddog out by the dump. "Everybody into the traces!" Maddog yelled.

Wouldn't you know it, the minute I put Jones in his harness, Jones rolled over on his back and kicked his feet in the air, like a cat, trying to claw his way out of his harness. "Jones," I hissed. "Stop that." Now he had dirt and straw and grass stuck all over his reindeer makeup and looked a mess. "You were supposed to work that sort of thing out of your system in stage rehearsal," I hissed at him. "Bad dog!"

"Take care of your reindeer!" Maddog snapped.

I helped Jones back to his feet and held him in place, much like hand-schooling a pup, and Jones stood there, not looking like much, then he curled his lip and growled, forced to look right in front of him, his kennel muzzle jammed into the butt of the dog in front of him, and I had a vision of a dog fight, right then and there, and that image was not refreshing nor stimulating. For a moment I had a picture of us bursting out before the crowded grandstands, closing night, Christmas Eve, dressed up like The Sherwood Forest Chinese Fire Drill Team and have an eight dog, dog fight. I watched the dog's tail move over slightly, and the dog's bunghole pucker and heard it go fizz-bleep. A moment later I said, "Geez!" I stood straight, punching Pooch The Mooch McGill on his arm. "You feeding garlic?" Jones looked at me, like why don't you ever grow up, like this is a nice place to visit, but when are we going home?

"Free ink, they call it," Maddog said, thumping on his big belly which was not padded one iota. I had to admit. He did make a nice Santa. "Ho! Ho! Ho!"

We all smiled and made small-talk remarks, like, "You look nice in your elf suit, Hugh." And Elsie said, "Hugh looks nice in three elf suits, all sewed together," and they stood there holding hands, and Little Elsie looked like she was drowning in her elf suit, it was about ten sizes too big, and it hung over her shoulders, and was all pulled up in lumps on her legs, and they made quite a pair, Hugh and Little Elsie. "Your big Greyhound looks nice," Little Elsie said, adjusting Jones' antlers, and I said, "Thanks," on behalf of Jones. Ben Dover was scratching his dog's ear telling him he was the nicest reindeer he had ever seen, and we all glowed with the comradery and the thought we were soon going to be in the spotlight on the track, thanks to Maddog McDermutt.

I was confident at this time this might work after all. We looked good dressed up in Elf suits. Maddog looked great behind his white beard, and his granny glasses didn't hurt the image any. And his Santa suit didn't look much different than his pink jump suit, and it struck me maybe his pink jump suit was a Macy's faded Santa suit anyway. And the bells on his hat tinkled, harmonized with the bells on the traces.

Maddog had thought of everything.

"Maddog," Fleas said. "I have to hand it to you. I think this time you have outdone yourself."

Maddog shrugged, modestly, stroked his fake beard, and went Ho! Ho! Ho! and for a moment there, I thought he really was Santa Claus, and then we could all hear the track announcer:

TEN MINUTES
BEFORE POST TIME
FOR THE NINTH RACE.

"OK Boys, that's the cue," Maddog said, and we all marched off for the track gate, where we stopped to wait.

I leaned forward and whispered in Pooch the Mooch's ear: "I think I have butterflies."

"Nerves and stage fright," Pooch said.

"Hold it down back there," Maddog said.

And we stood there, first on one leg, then the other, as the track announcer went on about this time of year and everybody's good feeling toward earth and mankind and all that and then the gate was open and in we went and Maddog stood on the back of the sled and yelled "MUSH" and I wanted to tell Maddog I thought the command was "ON DANCER, ON PRANCER," not "MUSH" and Maddog kept yelling "MUSH" like he was Sergeant Preston of the Yukon instead of Santa Claus, and the crowd applauded, obviously everybody was surprised, and we must have been quite a sight, eight Greyhounds dressed up like reindeer, right down to the antlers, and Santa on his sled, and his elves, all parading by, and waving, and good cheer and all of that, and I noticed out of the corner of my eye the mechanical lure sitting by the starting gate, or was it moving, I think it was moving, IT WAS MOVING, what was the rabbit doing right there, it should have been on the first turn hiding in the traps, it was RIGHT THERE, right off to Maddog's left, and it must have been A TEST between the Eighth and Ninth and the test wasn't finished, and we came in the gate a little early, and the dogs saw it too, and my heart sank because I knew what was next, and the dogs started barking, and the front dog lunged, then the dogs behind him lunged, Jones started bucking, trying to shake his harness, and all the dogs meant to have that lure, one way or the other, and that stupid reindeer grease-paint the dogs had on was like trying to wrestle greased watermelons, and the elves were having trouble, and the whole bunch humped away from them and down the track they went and Maddog hollering as they went by the finish line at about forty miles an hour "MER.......RY CHRISTMAS" and that dog sled fish-tailing back and forth behind the dogs and Maddog playing his part to the end yelling "GEE" and "HAW" and "WHOA" and "STOP YOU MISERABLE MULEHEADED SKUZBAGS" and it was obvious Maddog had no idea how to drive a dog sled or even how to brake one, and the lure went around the first turn and then the dogs went around the first turn.

Maddog did not.

Maddog did not negotiate the first turn. That dog sled came unhooked somehow from the dogs and made not the slightest indication it should turn and slammed into the first turn wall with a crash-bang-thud that could be heard downtown, eight bags of dog food exploding on impact and flying every which way.

I felt sick.

"Oh golly," Fleas said under his breath.

"Holy Jingle Bells," Pooch the Mooch McGill said. "Nobody could live through that."

Now here comes Santa's little reindeer team again, racing by, Jones in the middle, running and pulling as hard as he could, and I was proud of him for that, and everybody barking at the lure, their antlers swinging back and forth, past the tote board, around the far turn, harness bells dinging merrily as they raced by.

"I might win this one," Hugh Mungas said. "My dog's still in front."

"I think my dog Jones will finish somewhere in the middle," I said, trying to make light of what obviously was a very serious situation.

At the other end of the track, I could see movement. A red suit was climbing out of the wreckage. Maddog was alive!

The crowd applauded.

Maddog weaved about, stumbled, staggered here, staggered there, then stood erect and waved. He was brushing dog food out of his Santa beard.

He was OK!

The crowd applauded.

Boy we had 'em now. Maybe Maddog did minor in drama.

In a moment the leadout boys rushed out onto the track and all pitched in and picked up the horseshoed dog sled and hurried off with it. Maddog limped down the track, gathered up his elves, big grin on his face, and everybody went to slapping hands, and shaking hands, like we really did pull it off, and everybody waved at the crowd like Maddog had instructed, wave at somebody special, like a long-lost friend, a wink, a nod, a wave, then go the other way, clean across the grandstands, and pick somebody else and do it again, and that went on awhile. Finally, we all held hands and together we took a bow, like we meant for the first turn wreck as part of the script all the time, and in the end it was quite a show after all, and a darn good one I thought.

As we headed down the track, Maddog said, "Show biz, boys. Good old Show biz." We walked past the leadout boys, busy cleaning up the dog food mess on the first turn, brooms, dustpans, garbage bags, preparing the track for the next race.

Then we gathered up the team of dogs, all lined up at the lure trap, took off the antlers, led them off, hosed that Reindeer goop, whatever it was, off the dogs, walked them around for awhile, put them in the trailers where they could rest until we returned to the kennels. "Good job, Jones," I said, patting him on the head. "Well done." We trainers met at the rail, full of the Christmas spirit, like we had really done our part, and everybody bet the NUMBER FIVE dog in the third race, everybody chipping in, a community wager, on a dog called FROSTY'S SNOWMAN, which Maddog said could not possibly lose, not with a name like that on a night like this, and we all agreed. No way a dog with a name like that on a night like this could do anything but wish everybody a little good cheer, especially a gaggle of dog trainers who put on the best production this track had ever seen, written and produced and directed by Maddog McDermutt, and, in fact, the star himself, Maddog McDermutt.

FROSTY'S SNOWMAN ran dead last. By quite a bit.

"Oh well," Maddog said. "You can't win 'em all."

We all jumped in on that one.

"Merry Christmas, Boys," Maddog said.

"Merry Christmas, Maddog," we all joined in.

And it did not matter that FROSTY'S SNOWMAN ran last. It just did not matter.

"Now," Maddog said. "Guess who we're going to bet in the next race?"

I pulled out my program and opened it.

"Let me guess," I said, running my finger down the entries.

My scan came to rest on the NUMBER SEVEN dog.

"Maddog, you gotta be kiddin'," I said. "S.C.'S RUDOLPH?"

We all started reaching for our wallets, and we all handed over two bucks apiece to Fleas to go to the window and buy one big ticket for all of us.

As we waited for S.C.'S RUDOLPH to bring home in a big way the Christmas spirit to cap our evening, and I say that because S.C'S RUDOLPH was something of a long shot, Maddog said: "You know, boys, what I am going to do for Christmas? I am going to mail that dog sled to my godson, Fardington Maddog Worthington, out in Ulm, Montana."

"Well then," Fleas Finnegan said. "That'll be a surprise. Most kids want a set of soldiers. Or a train. Or a pony. But a dog sled that's bent in half. Think of it."

And so we all thought about it.

"Merry Christmas everybody," Maddog said.

"Merry Christmas," we all agreed.

I went to find a phone booth. After a few rings Sally said, "Hello?"

"Merry Christmas," I said.

"Merry Christmas," she said.

"How's your mother?" I asked.

"Fine. Did Jones run?"

"Well, sort of," I said. "We'll be home day after tomorrow."

TWELVE

Maddog had not been totally correct in his assessment of when I would return to Great Falls from Key West. One emergency after another seemed to pop up, and he said he could really use my help, and so Jones and I stayed on, and the days passed. Christmas came and went, then New Years. I helped Maddog close out Key West. Jones' papers never did show up. Everybody drove off to winter at the Yuma Greyhound track in Arizona; Jones and I flew home. Maddog told me he would pay me for my troubles when he caught up on his bills. If nothing else, I learned about racing Greyhounds and racing kennels. I was certain the experience was worth my returning to school a week late.

I had to admit, it was something of a letdown to be back to my ninth grade English teaching duties, Room 23, Paris Gibson Junior High. I was having trouble adjusting. A Greyhound race track existence was insane; that much I learned. The hours were impossible. Making a living at it was impossible. Working with the dogs themselves was impossible. The whole thing was stupid and impossible. Then why did I already miss it?

As I rearranged my desk from the stacks of papers the sub never corrected, papers of which I could not make head nor tail, I was glad to be back, lucky I had only missed a week of school. It could have been worse. I was convinced Maddog McDermutt was a certified fruit-cake lunatic. And maybe a liar to boot. I was not happy I never did get to see my dog run.

Before I even finished role, First Period had to hear the story of my adventures in Key West. The kids were polite, but insistent, that I bring Jones to school; they wanted to see a racing Greyhound, up close and personal.

And so I said I would. But only on the agreement that all week they would work hard on their compositions, do their dangling participle exercises, and the first fifteen minutes of Friday would be the fifty "S" words in the back of the literature book, not only spelling, but meaning. I received a few good-natured boos, but in general First Period agreed.

Between First and Second, out in the hall, a couple of teachers approached, asking, "Were you really racing Greyhounds in Key West?" I had to admit I was.

Period Two went down exactly like Period One. Bring the dog. Of course we will be good. For that we will be good. And they were. I even taught them a little English.

Mr. McNulty took his Greyhound to Key West, Florida.

Third period I retired to the faculty room, plopped my papers, grade book, and lesson plan book on the table. I was a week behind because I had been buns deep in dogs and dog racing, and I did not need Harry and Sheldon's canine expertise. I also did not need a grand inquisition. The principal came in, early I think, squeaked his chair, sat down, lit up.

I don't know why, I should have known better, but I asked Dr. Mayonaisse, who was, after all, my boss: "The kids were wondering if I would bring my racing Greyhound to school, this Friday, maybe talk about Greyhound racing. I was wondering if that would be all right."

The principal drew a deep drag. His eyes went around. "Write it down," he said.

"Sir?"

"Write it down."

"OK. Where?"

"In your lesson plans."

I thought about it.

"Why?"

"So if you are sick the substitute teacher will know what to do. Lesson plans are for substitutes when the regular teacher is sick."

"Sir," I said, "how can a sub know what to say about my dog."

"Exactly. That is what lesson plans are for. How else would a sub know what to say about your dog. So write it down. Objectives. Goals. Procedures."

"Yes sir." I moved my pen over to Friday and wrote:

BRING JONES
TALK ABOUT JONES

Done with that, I looked up, said, "You guys know who subbed for me last week?"

"Sure," Harry said. "Old friend of mine, retired math teacher. Your classes worked math problems all week."

So that's what was all over my desk.

"Your sub was in here Third Period with us, of course, and was very impressed with your lesson plans. He had no trouble at all following your instructions. Said you must be a great math teacher."

I looked at the principal. He was gone somewhere, behind a puff of smoke.

"Since you have such excellent lesson plans," Harry said, "it's only fair I have a copy of yours. So that I can see how it is done. So give me a copy of that one you're working on."

"Make it out in triplicate, would you?" Sheldon said.

I finished up my lesson plans as the bell to go to Fourth rang. I gave Harry and Sheldon a copy each; I picked up my pile of papers and books, headed for Fourth which went down exactly like First and Second. Bring the dog. Tell us about dog racing in Key West.

And so Friday morning rolled around, I kissed Sally goodbye, leashed up Jones, grabbed my briefcase, and headed for school. Jones had trouble with the school floor, nothing for his long nails to dig in to, so he kind of slipped and slithered his way down the hall, like a beginning, uncoordinated ice skater. The kids all oohed and awed and pointed. "Look at the big dog." "Is that a Greyhound?" "Hey, that's Mr. McNulty's big dog Jones." "Hey Jones, how's it going." And the dog slithered on.

The bell rang for First. The kids were all there, bright-eyed and bushy-tailed; nobody absent today. "Hey!" one kid said, "that's the same dog P'd on my lunch box." I took the roll, put up the attendance slip on the clip for the office aid to pick up, then turned to introduce the big guy Jones who had been standing patiently in the front of the room looking out over the class.

"And this," I said, "is Jones. Jones, can you say hello?"

And Jones barked, which in our small classroom, thundered.

What a remarkable dog!

Three kids fell out of their chairs; everybody chuckled. No harm done.

"Jones," I said, "is a racing Greyhound. He might be THE biggest racing Greyhound. I recently spent Christmas vacation, and then some, in Key West with 1,000 Greyhounds, and the biggest Greyhound I recall was 72 pounds. Jones weighs in at 102 pounds."

"Is he retired?" Bonnie, in the front of the room, asked.

"Yes," I said. "You could put it that way."

"How many races did he win?" Joe, to my left and half way down his row, asked.

"I'm not sure," I said.

"Is he famous?" Fred, over by the window, asked.

"Well not exactly. He's a house pet now."

"Yeah, but when he was running, was he any good?" Betsy, in back, asked.

"Of course he was," I lied. "He was one of the best."

"Where all'd he run?" Bert, from the middle, asked.

"I'm not sure," I said. "I do know he is from Australia. But let me tell you about his breed. His is the oldest breed of dog known. His ancestor's pictures are on the tombs of pharaohs in Egypt. For 2,000 years this dog and his ancestors have been bred for speed, to run down small game. The best in this breed can approach bursts of forty-seven miles per hour."

"Holy cow," Jennifer said.

"How fast can Jones run?" Alice asked.

"I'm not sure."

"Can he catch a rabbit?" Alex asked.

"Well, he never has, but I am sure he could if he wanted to."

The office aid opened the door, stepped in. As she reached up to pluck the attendance slip off its clip, she blew a big pink bubble, looked at me, looked at Jones. I pointed at my dog, said, "That, Young Lady, is Jones. Jones is my dog." Jones barked.

She looked at me. She looked at the dog. The bubble popped all over her face. She sucked, licked, sucked, in it went, more chewing, heavy on the left side. "If you say so," she said on her exit.

Second Period went along about the same as first. Third period Jones and I retired to the faculty room. I was surprised to see that Sheldon had his Irish setter Bobo the Great and Harry had his black lab Montana Black Satan in there. Sheldon said, smiling, "Just following our lesson plans."

I shook my head. The principal came in, sat down, lit up.

The dogs were busy sniffing each other over in the corner, tails straight up, circling, the usual. Sometimes I wished they wouldn't do that. "Sit!" Sheldon commanded, and the Irish setter sat. "Sit!" Harry commanded, and his black lab sat obediently. It was worth a try. "Sit!" I commanded in my best voice. Jones looked at me like I was an idiot.

"I haven't trained him to sit," I said.

"Really?" Sheldon said. "Could have fooled me."

"Have you trained him to do anything?" Harry asked.

"Well, he comes to me, when I call him. Usually. He'll give good chase to a jack rabbit. He barks when I ask him to."

The principal put out his cigarette, lit up his second. Jones came alongside of him, sniffed his pantleg. "Jones!" I said, sternly. "Jones don't do that."

Jones looked at me indifferently, saluted Dr. Mayonaisse's leg. The principal didn't seem to notice. Sheldon, all doubled up, had his head in his hands, convulsing. Harry, holding his stomach, had turned to look out the window. I pushed my chair back, stood up, looked down. Sure enough, the principal's leg was damp, a little puddle around his shoe. "Sir," I said.

"Yes, what is it?"

Harry shouted: "Get your stupid dog off my dog!"

I looked. Jones was attempting to mount Montana Black Satan in the corner of the room. The black lab was trying its best to stay obediently in a sit position. Jones had pushed Monty against the wall, slid him over on the slick floor. Harry tossed a book at Jones, hit him on the back. "Bad dog," I said, rushing over to grab my dog. "What's the matter with you?"

I snapped at Harry: "You don't have to throw things."

The principal arose and left to be the mystery guest somewhere else.

Sheldon broke up. He pointed at Harry's black lab, then grabbed his side. "I've never hurt so much in years," he said.

"I'm sorry," I said to Harry. "I had no idea your dog was in season. I thought Monty was a boy dog."

Harry said, "Monty is a boy dog."

"Oh," I said.

I could not think of anything else to say, except: "Bad dog, Jones. Bad."

The bell rang for Fourth. I leashed up Jones and headed down the hall for class; once again Jones had trouble with the hall floors, walked like one of those computer spiders humping itself along. Harry and Sheldon "HEELED!" their dogs in the opposite direction.

Once again I took roll, put the attendance slip on the wall clip, easy because everybody was all present and accounted for, and said, "Today, by popular request, I would like to talk about me and Jones."

Judy, in the middle of the room, raised her hand.

"Yes Judy," I said.

"Is not the preferred usage....Jones and me?"

What a perceptive ninth grader.

I thought for a moment, then answered:

"No," I said. "In this case it is me and Jones. As your English teacher, and where I've been, and with whom I have

156

done service, I tell you me and Jones is perfectly acceptable."

"Now then. Let me tell you about dipping for fleas in Key West, Florida........."

THIRTEEN

Several months later Jones and I went for a walk up the river, south of town. Jones and I had been looking for a rabbit up and down a few coulees, but we couldn't find one. I really didn't care if we found a rabbit for Jones to chase; it was a nice excuse to go for a walk. Jones shared the sentiment. If a rabbit did get up, I don't know that the big fellow would have given chase. He looked as relaxed as I. Had we spoiled him? Probably. Jones and I walked along, a lazy day, nice to be out and about. As long as we were in the general vicinity, I thought about running over to see Fard and the pups. "Want to drop by Fard's place?" I asked Jones.

Jones wagged his tail.

"Well then let's do it," I said, bending over to pat the dog on the back. "Let's head for the truck." Jones trotted on ahead.

I parked next to the WORTHINGTON mailbox, the swarm of flies buzzing a familiar welcome. I found Fard sitting, in the barn, hammering on a gizmo I recognized immediately: the dog sled from Key West, Maddog McDermutt's Christmas present to his godson.

Fard looked up. "Hello, Mr. McNulty."

"Fard," I said. "We were in the neighborhood, thought we'd drop in. How have you been?"

"All things considered, I guess I can't complain, Mr. McNulty. Hello, Jones."

Jones came up for a pat on the head.

"I think he likes you," I said.

Fard said, "He's a good dog. I like Jones, too."

Jones moved over to a bed of straw and sniffed around. My eyes were adjusting to the dark interior of the barn.

"Where'd you get the shiner, Fard?"

Fard hammered on a railing. "You know the old story about running into a door knob," he said.

"I'll bet some kid at school said the wrong thing, huh Fard? What's he look like?" Then I noticed a bruise on the top of Fard's hand. "Let me see that, Fard." I rolled up his sleeve. His arm was black and blue. "What's going on, Fard?"

"I'd rather not talk about it, Mr. McNulty. Would you like to help me with the sled?"

"Sure," I said. "What do you want me to do?"

"How about standing on the rail, there, put your weight on it, and I'll see if I can't pry that bent pipe straight."

I stood on the sled at the point Fard indicated. Fard took two 2 X 4's and wedged them between two struts. Then he hammered on the 2 X 4's, forcing the bent pipe to straighten. Satisfied, he said, "OK. Let's turn it over."

We both grabbed a runner, lifted, turned the sled over.

"Let's see if we can put the wheels to the axles," Fard said. I lifted the sled about a foot off the ground while he fitted the wheel, tightened down the nut. We did that for each wheel, stepped back to admire the infamous McDermutt sled.

"I have a bike pump around here somewhere," Fard said, walking along one wall, searching the corners.

"Here it is," I said, picking it up, handing it over.

I held the bike wheel steady while Fard pumped. The rubber tire fattened up, hardened.

"I think that's enough," I said, pinching the tire, and we moved on to the next tire, and worked our way around the sled.

"How's your mother, Fard?"

"Fine, Mr. McNulty. Thank you for asking."

Jones moved aside as Fard took a couple of swings with his hammer. "That one pipe won't go straight," Fard said. "Still has a kink in it. That must have been some kind of wreck my godfather Maddog McDermutt took on the first turn at Key West."

"That's putting it mildly," I said. "Do you plan to put the sled to use?"

"That possibility exists," Fard said.

I looked around the barn, poked my nose out the door and looked around. "Where are the pups and Miss Neopolitan?"

"Down to the river," Fard said, sitting on the front of the sled. "They usually go on down there this time of day."

"They're down on the river, Jones," I said.

Jones wandered out the barn.

"How are you getting along, Fard, I mean since your dad passed away. Is everything all right?"

"We're short on money," Fard said. "But then we always were. Mother had a job in Cascade, but she lost it. Father had no insurance, but he did have foresight with the maggots in the mailbox. I caught enough whitefish to feed the pups for another two months, maybe more, and there are more maggots where they came from, so for the moment dog food is no problem."

"Well that's good, Fard."

I went to the barn door, looked out. Jones ambled along through the cottonwoods, headed for the river. A car swerved off the bypass in a screeching cloud of dust, one tire slamming into the ditch, the car bouncing, crowhopping, careening down the Worthington driveway, skidding to a stop, the front fender slamming into the gate.

Mrs. Worthington threw open the door, fell out, picked herself up, dusted herself off. She saw me.

"Oh hi there," she said, staggering over.

A Montana Highway Patrol car turned off the bypass, moved on down the Worthington driveway, parked behind Mrs. Worthington's car.

I noticed Fard continued to work on the dog sled.

A patrolman stepped out of his car, walked up to Mrs. Worthington's car, reached in the window to retrieve her keys. As he walked over to us, he pulled the car key off the ring, handed the rest of the keys to Mrs. Worthington. "Mrs. Worthington," he said, "I don't know what we're going to do with you. You have two D.W.I.'s; the judge took away your drivers' license; and here we are again. What remains is to toss you in jail and throw away the key until you dry out."

Mrs. Worthington straightened herself. "Are you insinuating....."

The patrolman looked in the barn. "Hi Fard," he said. Fard waved.

To Mrs. Worthington, he said, "I'm going to keep this key. I don't want to catch you driving again. I expect to hear you are attending Alcoholics Anonymous and receiving counseling as the judge ordered."

Mrs. Worthington belched, swaggered off to the house. She paused at the mailbox, and a great cloud of black flies gave her the effect of a halo. "Tell that little jerk in the barn some people want to buy those worthless dogs for research, and we could use the money."

She moved on into the house.

I walked the patrolman to his car. "Maybe it is not for me to say," I said, "but I think maybe the old lady is beating up on Fard, physical abuse."

"Wouldn't surprise me," the patrolman said. "And you are?"

"Oh. Sorry. Ryan McNulty. I teach English at Paris Gibson Junior High in Great Falls. I have a racing Greyhound. That's how I know Fard."

"I see." The patrolman sat behind the wheel, looked at the barn. "If I didn't think the old lady would sauce the money, I'd suggest selling that litter of pups. Worthless mixed litter, I hear."

"Oh I don't know about that," I said. "Fard's catching fish to feed them."

"Problem is," the patrolman said, "the kid isn't going to school regularly. Half the time he's truant."

The car radio crackled, then a message I couldn't understand.

The patrolman said, to me, "Call's for me. I'm outta here."

I walked back to the barn as the patrol car drove on up to the bypass. Fard sat in the middle of a pile of harness.

I grabbed one end, and the two of us worked on untangling it. "Here," I said. "This way. No. Under. That's it." We had it now. The traces stretched clear across the barn, brought back memories, of Key West, of Maddog, of Greyhound racing. I could smell what Maddog called reindeer liniment on the harness.

Fard piled the harness neatly, set it on the dog sled.
"Looks nice, Fard," I said.

"Mr. McNulty, can you keep a secret?"

"I'd sure try, Fard," I said.

Fard went to the back of the barn, felt around under a board, brought forth an envelope. He opened it, handed over the contents.

I looked them over: Five registration papers.

"Fard," I said, "you registered the pups?"

"The Greyhounds, yessir, Mr. McNulty, I did. Everything is in order, and we are ready to proceed."

"No questions with registration about a mixed litter?"

"Who said anything about a mixed litter," Fard said.

I thought about it. Sure. Why mention it in the first place. "That's pretty smart, Fard. You didn't lie."

"Exactly."

"You know, Fard, I have never received papers on Jones. Maddog keeps saying they're in the mail."

Fard said, "Dog trainers give dogs away, but they never follow up with the papers. That way the man on the street can't cheapen the breed with stupid crosses."

"You mean to tell me Maddog McDermutt has the papers on my dog and never intended to give them to me?"

"That's about the size of it, Mr. McNulty."

"Well, we'll see about that," I said.

Jones stood outside, looking in.

"Couldn't find them?" I asked Jones.

Fard and I walked out the barn, stopped at my truck. Fard said, "Before you go, Mr. McNulty, I have something to ask you."

"Yes Fard?"

164

"Mr. McNulty, I have been in touch with my godfather Mr. McDermutt, who as you know is now racing in Yuma, Arizona. He has asked me to approach you on the possibility of running your own kennel at the Black Hills Greyhound Track in Rapid City this summer. As a school teacher, Mr. McNulty, you would have the time to accept such a proposal, although you would have to miss school the month of May. My godfather told me that all the dogs are doing very well in Yuma, within all the kennels, and everybody is willing to stake you with graded dogs and pups. I would really be interested in that, Mr. McNulty, and would seriously consider letting you break in my Greyhounds."

Fard paused to let all that sink in. Me? Run my own kennel? I had all of two weeks experience in Key West.

Fard could read minds. He said, "Maddog said that he and his associates would help you with everything. They have too many dogs as it is. One more kennel would really help. Do you think you could find it within yourself, Mr. McNulty, to take a booking at Rapid City this summer?"

At this moment, as if on cue, here came the troops up from the river, through the cottonwoods, up the lane, eight enthusiastic pups of various statures and strides, racing right at us, suddenly digging in to stop, buns over teakettles, stumbling, rolling, growling, biting; good golly they had grown; Miss Neopolitan stopped alongside Jones, and they stood side by side, watching. Miss Neopolitan looked a little haggard. I could well imagine this group applying stress to mother. I reached down and rolled a chow chow on his back; he playfully bit me, growling, full of it. I patted each pup, then once more all around. Two chow chows, the wolf, the Greyhounds. All right, fine, once more all around. I wondered what it would

165

be like to have that kind of energy. They suddenly raced for the barn door, under and around the legs of Jones and Miss Neopolitan, and they could be heard rough-housing it in there, growls, squeals, grunts, cries.

"Fard," I said. "Let me think on it a little. I want to talk to the wife. I also want to talk to Maddog." I looked at Jones. "Do you think I could run Jones at Black Hills?"

"Mr. McNulty, that is between you and my godfather. You'll have to secure Jones' papers."

"Fard, if his royal highness Mr. McDermutt comes across with Jones' papers so that he can race too, I'll think about it. Are you all right out here?"

"We're going to make it, Mr. McNulty. One way or the other, we're going to make it."

"How about school, Fard. You can't miss school."

"Mother is not going to sell the dogs to research. If I have to miss school on that account, that's the way it goes."

"Give me a call if you need something, Fard."

Fard patted Jones on the back. "See you later, Jones."

As I drove for home, the thought of Fard losing his litter of pups haunted me. I looked over at Jones, nonchalantly gazing out the window, watching the prairie go by. Nothing seemed to bother him. Later at home I told Sally all about it.

The next day in class, who knows why, I asked the kids what they thought. I explained that if I took the Rapid City booking I would have to leave in May and stick them with a sub again, and I really did not want to do that. I liked them; they liked me; we were having a great year. The response was unanimous and overwhelming:

"Mr. McNulty. Run the dog. You can teach school the rest of your life. Go run the dog."

"We want Jones to run the race track."

And class after class, as if they had a script, somebody would get caught up in the idea and would start a chant: "Run Jones! Run Jones! Run Jones!"

I shushed each class, one after the other. By the end of the day the message was in the halls, in the classes, in the faculty room, in the parking lot after school. The message was clear. Run Jones.

At the teachers' mailboxes I ran in to that counselor, what's-her-name, and she had to ask: "Are you really going to run Jones?"

I said, "I haven't made up my mind yet."

"Let me know when you do," she said. "By the way there is going to be a general inquiry Monday night at a school board work session on that book we were discussing."

"Of Mice and Men? You're still worried about Of Mice and Men? Lady, count me out. I'm busy Monday night."

She made a notation on her clipboard. "I'll pass that on," she said, marching off.

I ran into the department chairman on the way out the building. I asked: "Did somebody say we had a class set of Salinger's Catcher in the Rye?"

"Well," Sally said, after I explained my day to her. "You'd better write Black Hills and take that booking. And you'd better make sure you have the papers on Jones. It's only for the summer."

I gave her a big hug.

I phoned Fardington Maddog Worthington. "Fard," I said, "I haven't talked to Maddog or the South Dakota track yet, but I have decided to run my own kennel. I would consider it an honor if you would let me break in your pups. What the heck, bring the wolf and chow chows too. And Miss Neopolitan."

And Fard said, "I was hoping beyond hope you would take that booking, Mr. McNulty. And thank you so much for the offer. You can rest assured, we will support you 100 per cent. I am prepared to lease my five Greyhounds and Miss Neopolitan to you for 35 per cent. We'll work something out on the wolf and two chow chows. We'll be there."

Then I phoned Maddog McDermutt in Yuma.

"Maddog," I said, "I have been visiting with Fard Worthington. I have decided to take you up on your offer of a booking at Rapid City."

"Oh good," Maddog said. "That's wonderful. I'll tell everybody here. We have plenty of dogs here for you to run. Graded dogs. Pups."

"Maddog, I will be breaking in Fard's five Greyhound pups."

"Sounds good to me. You can count on me to race them after Rapid City. If they're as good as their breeding, they'll go on to run the big apple."

"And Fard said I could race Miss Neopolitan."

"Oh she's a dandy," Maddog said. "She's older of course, had a litter of pups, but at Black Hills she's good enough to make you some money, help pay the bills. She's a good, steady campaigner, that's for sure."

"And Jones? Maddog, I plan to run Jones."

"Oh that's wonderful," Maddog said. "Simply wonderful."

"You'll have to find the papers on him, Maddog."

"What's that?"

"Papers, Maddog. P.A.P.E.R.S. Read my lips. Remember, you gave Jones to me when the Great Falls track closed. I don't have registration papers on Jones. Jones can't run without papers."

"I'll see what I can do," Maddog said.

"Not good enough, Maddog. No Jones. No deal," I said. "And that's final."

Then I phoned the Rapid City Black Hills Greyhound Track. The booking contract, I was told, would be in the mail tomorrow. All I had to do was agree to list a few graded dogs (Miss Neopolitan to name one) and list a few pups, whatever Maddog and the rest of the Yuma bunch tossed in, as well as Fard's, although I was sure Fard's pups were not old enough to run Rapid until the end of the season, in August. School them in really well, then knock 'em dead. "Well, Jones," I said to my dog, snoring on the couch, "this summer both of us have jobs. Time to pay some bills."

"Sally!" I hollered around the corner, "you want to help me run a racing Greyhound kennel this summer in Rapid? We'll look at it as something of a vacation."

"Sure," she said. "Why not."

I leaned over and scratched the big dog's ears. He grunted contentedly. I said, "You're going to get your chance, Jones."

The next day in Third Period prep, Harry, Sheldon and Dr. Mayonaisse were reassuring.

"You gotta be kidding," Harry said.

"You're nuts," Sheldon said.

"Turn in your lesson plans," Dr. Mayonaisse said.

FOURTEEN

Winter passed quickly into spring. My classes worked on spelling, vocabulary, grammar; they wrote papers, read stories, gave speeches. I had not been officially observed by administration yet, but I anticipated that event any day, and I even looked forward to it. I hoped it would not be Dr. Mayonaisse, but the department chairman whom I had come to regard as a good English teacher. When you're good, you want to be recognized. I was good. Every week I wrote out daily lesson plans, and daily I ignored them. I forced myself not to worry about Maddog, how he and the other trainers were faring in Yuma. I had agreed to run a kennel in Black Hills. I would see the crew again soon enough. I walked Jones every day now, and twice a day on the weekends, shaping up the big boy for the track. The kids continued to ask about him. Jones was indeed going to run this summer at Black Hills.

Run Jones!

That time was coming, but how fast was Jones? Really?

That thought nagged at me, from time to time. He had yet

to show me he could catch a rabbit. Frequently, he would chase one. Never had he caught one.

In the middle of March I received a note from Maddog McDermutt.

Dear Ryan,

We have talked of you often in Yuma. Looking forward to working with you in Rapid. I have been unable to generate papers on Jones. I'm afraid he will not be able to run Black Hills. Sorry.

As Ever,

Maddog

I composed a terse response.

Dear Maddog:

No Jones? No Ryan and Sally. Suggest you find Jones' papers.

Regards,

Ryan and Sally McNulty

I hadn't been back from the mailbox more than five seconds when Sally announced: "Fardington Worthington calling. Collect."

"Well, it's only twenty cents or something from Ulm," I said. "I have been wondering how he has been doing." I picked up the phone, accepted the call from the operator. "Fard," I said. "What can I do for you?"

"Mr. McNulty," Fard said. "You won't believe how much the pups have grown."

"I'll bet," I said. "How's the wolf?"

"Magnificent, Mr. McNulty. Absolutely magnificent."

"That's wonderful, Fard."

"Mr. McNulty, I insist you come out and see the pups."

I held the phone aside, with my hand over the mouthpiece, and said to Sally: "Fard invited us out to see the pups. Want to drive to Ulm?"

"Right now?"

"Sure. Why not."

"OK Fard. Thanks for the invite. We're on our way."

We said our good-byes and hung up. Sally, Jones and I piled into the truck and headed for Ulm.

"Beautiful day, eh?" I said.

"Lovely," Sally said.

And it was, too.

We pulled up alongside the fly-infested WORTHINGTON mailbox and piled out the truck. A great black swarm, agitated, buzzed and fussed. Fard hollered from the barn, stepped out and waved, and we waved, walked over. Out the door here they came, rushing, playful, heads back and laughing, five gray brindle Greyhound puppies, two Chinese chow chows, and a wolf, all falling over each other, all racing to see who could reach our feet first. Miss Neopolitan followed,

173

wagging her tail. She and Jones touched noses.

"Is that a litter or is that a litter?" Fard asked.

The pups growled, rolled around, raced around our legs and nipped at our pantlegs, delighted in general to see us.

"I'll say," I said, looking over the wolf puppy, a tough-looking hombre. "His eyes are yellow."

Sally looked a chow chow in the eye. "This one's eyes are blue."

"I think they change as they grow older. I guess. I don't know. These mixed litters are amazing, eh Fard?"

Fard said, "Who wants a dog half chow chow and half Greyhound? What are the options on a wolf and Greyhound cross? One of the kids down at school said his father said owning a wolf, or a wolf cross, was illegal."

"Fard," I said. "Things have a way of working out."

I looked around the yard, past the barn, down through the cottonwoods. "Where did Jones go?" I asked.

"Fard," I said, "Can you afford to feed all these dogs, day after day?"

"As I told you, Mr. McNulty, the fishing has been great. I set lines in the river. The whitefish season is over, but I have been having good luck recently with suckers and carp. There are some big fish in the Missouri River, Mr. McNulty."

"I'll bet I know what you use for bait," Sally said.

"I fish with maggots, Mrs. McNulty," Fard said. "Bottom feeders love maggots. In fact I have some extra fish: would you like to try a carp or sucker with Jones there?"

"No Fard," I said. "Jones is stuck on canned and dry dog food. Thanks anyway."

174

Fard patted Miss Neopolitan on the head, said, "Mother was approached the other day by two men who wanted to buy the dogs for research. Mother said they were even interested in Jones."

"What!" I said.

Sally stepped in. "Over my dead body, Fard."

Well I was proud of her right then. Took the words right out of my mouth. "Fard," I said, reaching for my wallet, "We would like to make a little contribution, in case you need a little something." I handed over two twenties.

"That's very thoughtful of you, Mr. and Mrs. McNulty. Thank you. That will help out a great deal."

"Our pleasure, Fard," I said for the both of us.

Jones ambled on over. Fard scratched him behind the ear. "Besides," Fard said, grinning, "isn't it about time we all see the big fellow here go around? What do you say, Jones?"

Jones wagged his tail. The wolf pup jumped up and down with lots of kisses for Jones. Then all the pups were jumping up and down. Jones seemed embarrassed by the whole thing.

"Did my godfather Maddog McDermutt send you the registration papers on Jones?"

"No," I said. "Not yet."

"I'll talk to Godfather about it," Fard said.

Sally, Jones and I piled in the truck. For a minute there, I thought *you, me, the dog, forever* had been burned into the windshield.

But it was only a reflection.

FIFTEEN

Saturday morning, two days into May after a very rainy April, it was finally Chinooking again. I was in the kitchen. When I finished my coffee, cookies, and the paper, I planned to take Jones for a walk up a coulee, look for a rabbit to course. Jones and I had been going out every day; jacks were hard to find. Jones had given many chases but hadn't caught one yet.

I looked under the table, then around the corner into the hall. "Where is Jones?" I asked Sally, washing up the breakfast dishes.

"His lordship is on his usual throne, the couch, taking his morning Z's."

The phone rang. I answered. "Hello?"

"Collect call from Fard Worthington."

"Yes Operator, I'll accept the charges."

Sally looked over from the sink. I mouthed "FARD" to her, and pointed in the direction of Ulm. She nodded.

"Hello, Mr. McNulty," Fard said, "greetings and a nice warm Chinook, eh? Also, Mr. McNulty, a belated Happy Easter to you."

"Well thank you, Fard," I said, "and same same and many more to you."

"Mr. McNulty, I am happy to report that the dog sled Godfather McDermutt sent me for Christmas has been totally repaired; you will recall the old kill-two-birds-with-one-stone saying; I thought perhaps you and your wife would like to see not only the sled but how the pups are doing. I'm very proud of their progress. I know they are looking forward to actual race track training in your kennel this summer."

"Well Fard, that certainly is a generous invitation; hold on a minute and let me check with the wife." I put the phone down, addressed Sally, stoic at the sink. "Say, Fard Worthington has invited us out to see his new dog sled and the pups. Want to drive on out to Ulm and check it out?"

"Sure," Sally said, turning off the tap. "Why not. It's a nice day for a drive. Right now?"

"I'll ask," I said, and returned to the phone, and to Fard, I asked, "Right now?"

"Sure," Fard said. "Any time is fine."

"Well, let's say about a half hour, more or less?"

"Fine."

"See you then."

And I hung up the phone. That was really nice. "Hey, Jones, you lazy mutt," I yelled to my big brindle Greyhound, "We're going out to Ulm to see the pups." I poked my head around the corner.

One eyelid popped up; the eye blinked, looked at me; the eyelid closed. The dog groaned, rolled over, his back to me, the ratty Greyhound tail hanging off the couch and touching the floor.

"You'll have to carry his lazy buns to the truck," Sally said. "I swear, I have never seen such a worthless creature. He does absolutely nothing except eat and sleep."

"And chase rabbits," I reminded her.

"I think the rabbit population is safe with him around," Sally said.

I walked over and poked the dog. "Come on, Jones, we're going to Ulm, to see the pups. And Miss Neopolitan." Jones raised his head, looked around the room, at me, then at Sally, snapped off a quick window-slammer, then hopped off the couch. Sally held the door open for him, and the giant Greyhound sauntered on out, down the lane, saluted the birch tree in the front yard, then Sally held the truck door open, Jones jumped up and in; we were in; and we were off for Ulm.

Jones sat between Sally and me on the pickup seat, panting lightly, watching the traffic, and whatever, the big Greyhound towering over both Sally and me. He had to stoop forward, and bend his neck, to see out the window. Powerful shoulders, no knobs on the backbone, no ribs. He had come in to his own, solid muscle. One thing we McNultys knew how to do: feed the dog. Feed the big, strong dog and make the big, strong dog bigger and stronger. He might not have been fast in his days at the track because he was too big, and now he was bigger, but no matter: this old boy did not take garbage off anybody, or anything, man or beast, flora or fauna. The big fellow passed a little gas, and I said to Sally, having caught the awful, nose-curling fragrances first, a silent but deadly (SBD), rolling down my window all the while, and I said it as pleasantly as I could, I really did: "Would you mind rolling down your window, Dear, I think Jones did a bad thing."

And now the SBD was upon her, and her nose contorted, and her eyes started to water, and down the window came.

"Whew!" she said. "Whew!"

what you need, McNulty, is a dog

I elbowed Jones on his powerful shoulder. "Stop that SBD stuff, Jones," I said, and the dog gave me a big wet kiss, the kind when you least expect it, slurp and you've been had, and wiping my face with my sleeve, I have to report the dog's breath wasn't much better than the gasses produced on the other end. I spit out the window three times. The dog smiled. I kid you not, Jones smiles. One lip goes up, his eyes twinkle, and he smiles. Then he passes gas. "You stink like something dead for three weeks," I said.

"Stinks is a kind assessment," Sally said. "I think there is something seriously wrong with Jones. No wonder that McDermutt fellow gave him to you. Who'd want a dog with a habit like that?" Jones grunted, yawned, his halitosis permeating everything.

Sometimes I found my dog repulsive.

Of course my main reason for visiting the Worthingtons was to take a look at Fard's litter. I was anxious to work with the pups and school them in for Fard.

Apparently, Miss Neopolitan was a little on the promiscuous side, well no, even the late Mr. Worthington had raved on in his last moments about how the dog had been all over the neighborhood, let's be honest. I mean the chow chows down the road, that was one thing; but a wolf?

"What's it been?" I asked Sally. "October? The pups must be six months old by now."

"Something like that," Sally said.

Jones saw several cows standing along the road and barked directly in my ear which sent my head to ringing.

"You block-headed dog," I hissed. "No. No kisses. You think you want to kiss me after where you've been? You settle down."

Sally gave me a look, like nobody's going to kiss me either, you or the dog, then turned her head out the window again. "The odor doesn't go away, does it," she said.

"That may not have been the dog," I had to confess. "Those cookies you baked, which I have been eating hand and fist yesterday and this morning, should be sent to NASA as formula for rocket fuel."

"Is that so," Sally said.

I turned off Interstate 15, drove along the bypass for about a mile, turned down the lane and parked in front of Fard's house. I beeped the horn. The black cloud of flies erupted, buzzed up and around the WORTHINGTON mailbox. By the time we were out of the truck, Fard was down the walk. He shook my hand. "Mr. McNulty, how nice to see you again. Mrs. McNulty. And Jones." He shook my wife's hand, patted Jones on the head.

"Thanks for coming out," Fard said.

"Thanks for inviting us," I said.

We watched Jones salute the mailbox; the flies protested magnificently, a great black swarm. Then Jones ran to the barn door and barked.

"He knows who's in there," Fard said.

"Smart dog," I said.

"Good guess," Sally said.

The first to walk out the door to greet Jones was, in size, his equal, maybe not intellectually, but certainly physically. Jones touched noses with the wolf pup, who immediately became subservient, running around, touching noses, sniffing butt, tail up and wagging, growling, the hair on his back standing on end. Clearly the dominant canine.....Jones. Then both critters looked at us, wagged their tails; the wolf broke into a trot, as though he had folks to see and places to go and bills to pay, off into the cottonwoods down by the river, and Jones ran off with him. Jones turned it on, found another gear, and the wolf pup was right there, loping along.

"Wow," I said. "That's something else. You don't suppose we could shave him and run him as a Greyhound at Black Hills?"

"I don't think he has the Greyhound's head," Fard said.

"You'll have trouble finding a racing muzzle for a head like that. Secondly, I don't think he'd fit in the starting boxes."

"I suppose," I said.

"That wolf pup is magnificent," I said to Sally. "You can see a little Greyhound in him, in the chest and the hindquarters, but he is without a doubt a wolf. And he's so big."

"Beautiful animal," Sally said.

"Wolves are big," Fard said.

"Prairie wolves?" I said. "Fard, not that big."

"Timber wolf," Fard said. "The father was making his

way to Yellowstone Park, from Canada and Glacier Park, leastwise that's the story from Montana Fish and Game."

"Wow," I said. "Life has its little twists, doesn't it. Almost every day you read about wolves in Montana, sightings here, sightings there, letters to the editor in the paper on both sides, some want wolves, some don't, all kinds of lip service given to the mysterious wolf, and here you have one in your barn. I think it can very safely be said Montana has wolves."

"Very good, Mr. McNulty," Fard said.

Sally raised an eyebrow at me, as if to say she did not care for the precocious answer. I nodded. No big deal. Besides, Fard didn't mean it that way.

Next out of the barn tumbled the two Chinese Chow Chows, into a puppy fight, rolling, growling, playfully biting, then up and tearing around in a circle, elongated Chinese Chow Chows. They looked like Chow Chows in the bow and in the stern, but midship was all Greyhound, deep chests, powerful shoulders, tucked up bellies, a strange-looking cross I thought. They were good size too, but nothing compared to the wolf. They took a look at us, wagged their strange, curlycue tails, then headed for the river. They could up and hightail it too.

And now here came the fawn Miss Neopolitan and her five Greyhound pups: all brindle.

The Greyhounds took off for the river, loping, bumping shoulders, then they saw the Chow Chows off in the cottonwoods, and they put everything into high gear, and they could run.

"Wow!" I said. "Those guys can pick 'em up and put 'em

down. They can really move it. Schooling those pups in at Black Hills will be a real treat I bet, eh Fard?"

"Bred in the purple," Fard said.

Under her breath, and I'm sure Fard did not hear her, my wife said, "And the red, and the yellow, and the blue, and the pink..."

I poked her and she quit.

"Well, I'd like to show you the dog sled Godfather McDermutt sent me," Fard said. "I painted it."

"Great," I said. "Let's have a look."

We walked around the barn, and there it was, sure enough, the Key West dog sled.

With balloon bike wheels.

A dark blue.

"It is my intention to train the pups to pull this dog sled," Fard said.

"Why would you want to do that?" my wife asked.

I jumped right in: "My experience with racing Greyhounds amounts to one dog, Fard, but I find the breed to be exceptionally intelligent. I'll bet it would be fun. I would be interested in the results."

"You're beginning to sound like him," Sally whispered in my ear.

Fard held up a coil of leather straps and buckles and snaps. "These are the traces," Fard said. "I soaped them down until they look and feel like new."

And here came the dogs up from the river, stretched out, bumping shoulders, racing each other with every thing they had, all spread out, racing for the barn. Miss Neopolitan and the wolf were in front, but not by much. Then the Greyhound pups. Then the Chow Chows.

"Where's Jones?" I said.

"Here he comes now," Sally said, pointing to the river.

Jones was really flying up the lane. "Must have been distracted," I said. Or, I said, jokingly, "He wanted to give the rest of 'em a handicap."

The dogs milled around, tongues hanging out, chests heaving, panting. They were Greyhounds, throughout. The deep chests, the long legs, the way they ran up the lane, stretched out, heads down, back legs reaching beyond the front legs, backs arching, driving. The wolf had a greater stride, more of a lope; the chow chows seemed stockier, more powerful, but equally as fast.

"If we can place these pups on the roster at Black Hills at the end of the season, Fard, I think we might win some races and make some money."

"I certainly hope so, Mr. McNulty."

"Remember this sled from Key West?" I asked Jones.

Jones growled.

"I think he does," I said. "Well, let's give it a try."

I grabbed Jones by his collar and led him over to Fard who put a leather harness on him, snapped it together, threw the rest of the harness in the sled, then walked to the back of the sled, grabbed both handles, stood on the little platform on the back of the sled, and hollered: "Mush!"

Nothing.

"Mush!" Fard said.

Jones turned around to look at him.

I walked to the front of the sled, grabbed Jones's collar, but he growled at me, and I let go. "Don't you growl at me, Jones," I said. "Bad dog." I shook a finger at him. I really meant it.

On reflection I think Jones felt a little foolish in the harness, that's all, and in a minute we were all caught up in the moment, grabbing dogs. Sally had a Chow Chow. I had Miss Neopolitan. Fard had a Greyhound pup, bucking and crowhopping, then standing still to look us over with eyes wide. We grabbed the rest, another Chow Chow, and the other Greyhounds, and then we all stood and looked at the wolf. I for one was not going to grab the wolf. Nobody else was moving very fast in his direction, either. Fard said, "Here boy." And the big critter with yellow eyes strode over to his master's side, and Fard put him into harness, and we all stood back and admired our work. And there they were. Jones in front, then Miss Neopolitan, then five Greyhound pups, then the chow chows, then the wolf, then the sled, then the big moment. Fard took his place on the little step at the back of the sled and yelled "MUSH!!!!" and absolutely nothing at all happened.

"Well," I said, looking over the sled and team. "Why don't I lead Jones around a little, and the rest should follow."

"Capital, Mr. McNulty," Fard said.

"Come on, big boy," I said to Jones, tugging on his collar. "Let's go for a walk, and don't you growl at me."

And everything began to move forward. Sally applauded. "Why don't you jump aboard," I said, nodding to the sled. Sally shrugged, like why not that could be fun, then seated herself in the middle of the sled, and up the road we went, the dogs all moving along in single file, and soon we were on the bypass blacktop, and a car went by and some smart aleck yelled, "What'a ya think this is, Alaska?" and then another car went by, slowed, and two faces peered out, one said, "What do we have here?" and then the car moved on, and I started to trot a little, caught up in the excitement of it all; it really was a clever, unique thing this dog sled on wheels, and now a pickup truck pulled up alongside, and it had an Irish Setter in the back, looked like Sheldon's Irish Setter, and the driver wanted to know where the Stiggerdorfs lived, the ones with the Irish Setter kennels, because his Irish Setter in the back there couldn't be in season more; she was having such a heat flash her thermostat was about to explode, and the driver laughed at his own good humor, and I laughed, good sport, even though I thought the comment a touch crude, and I felt Jones straighten up under my hand, and he sniffed and sniffed some more, and his ears went up, and he was staring at that Irish Setter in the back of the truck, and the Irish Setter barked, and Jones about crawled out of his skin, and I don't know if he barked or growled, it was kind of a gargley whine, and the wolf behind me howled, and that sent a shiver up my spine, and Fard shouted to the driver where the Stiggerdorfs lived, "about a half mile down the road, then turn right;" the truck pulled away; Jones was right there keeping pace, and I had a good hold of his collar, but I couldn't keep up this trot much longer, and so I broke into a run, and now the dog sled was moving right along, the bike wheels made for blacktop, al-though maybe a couple of them could use a little oil, and

Fard shouting something like "not too fast to begin with Mr. McNulty," and I was having trouble putting one leg in front of the other, and I wished that truck would speed up and go down the highway and that stupid Irish Setter and her big brown eyes, fluttering eyelids, slobbering kisser; and Jones..... now Jones gargled again never taking his eyes off her, and he was lunging against my hand, and I couldn't help it, I took a header right there on the pavement, and I rolled to see the dogs go by, the wolf crowhopping and bucking and howling on by, and then I watched Sally go by, and she had hold of the dog sled with both hands (she did not look one bit pleased), and then Fard went by yelling "Whoa! Whoa! Whoa!" and then "Stop you fools!" and the truck turned off the bypass onto what I presumed to be the Stiggerdorf's, and the sled was full steam now, and I watched the dogs, Jones in the lead, take a 90 degree turn, but the sled unfortunately did not have that capacity, and it kept going on down the road, and everything must have come apart, because the dogs kept following the pickup, and the sled went on down the road for about a hundred and fifty yards before the road turned, and the sled didn't, and the sled vanished in the borrow pit; Fard jumped clear; the last part of it I saw was the back of my wife's head, and Fard looking down into the borrow pit, and Jones was at the back of the truck, and I was on my feet, running, yelling, "Watch out for that big dog! Be careful! Hey! Jones, don't you do that!" The whole string of dogs jerked forward as Jones had hold of the Irish Setter, and he had pushed her up against the truck, and I couldn't run any faster, and the Irish Setter yelped, and all the dogs started howling, and I felt sick all over, and by the time I reached the truck, the driver was standing next to the dogs, the man's face all contorted, like he wanted to have a coronary but couldn't, and in my judgment at the time he was not a happy man, and his Irish Setter looking over her shoulder, fearfully, at the giant Greyhound who had another nine dogs tied to him, and Jones with a stupid look on his face, like this was the bad part, like he ought to be doing something, and he didn't know for sure what, and the owner of the house came out with a bucket of water and threw it on Jones, and the two dogs came unstuck, and now the wolf started to howl, and that sent a chill up my back, and now the owner of the house wanted to know what all the dogs were doing in his driveway and then everybody took in to howling along with the wolf, but finally they all wound down. I backed off, led Jones off, everybody else following; they had little choice. The Irish Setter sat down next to the front tire to watch, not knowing whether to be flattered, shocked, or pleased, or all three, and so she sat there wondering about it, like dogs do wonder, and I went up the driveway and headed for the Worthington place, and Fard and Sally came along, pushing the sled which didn't look too much the worse for wear, and we made our way back down the blacktop, down Fard's road, to the barn. This time Sally walked along with nothing to add, not one word, not even half a word or any part of a word, and we unleashed all the dogs, and I told Jones to jump in the truck, and I waved to Fard and said thanks for everything, had a good time, nice seeing you, thanks for having us out, say hello to your mother for us, and good luck with the pups, and backed up the road and up onto the bypass, and by the time we had reached Interstate Freeway I-15, Jones was snoring on the seat, between us, dead to the world.

"What's he so tired for?" Sally asked.

"I don't think you saw the half of it," I said. "You were in the ditch. You are all right, aren't you?"

"Sure," she said. "Nothing fifteen chiropractors can't fix over the next ten years."

We rolled down our windows.

"I am so excited about Jones running the track I can't sit still," I said. "In my view Jones is, maybe with a little schooling, the fastest dog in the world. I'd like to see the dog, any dog, that could run with Jones. Might as well win a few bucks with him at the track. Eventually, a derby here, a stakes race there. Why not. Might as well strike while the iron is hot, as they say."

Was that what Maddog McDermutt had meant? You, me, the dog? Did he know all along that I would bring this Grade E reject to future greatness?

"Dear," I said. "Like I said before. Black Hills will be like a vacation. I think you'll really enjoy dog track life."

"It'll be a second honeymoon," she said. "The two of us locked up in a room with forty racing Greyhounds, all passing obnoxious gasses from the special feeding formulas of Maddog McDermutt. It'll be heaven."

Well that hurt.

Another mile down the road Sally redeemed herself. She said, "I have a confession to make. I want to see Jones run, too."

190

I felt better already. I could hear my class chanting. Run Jones! Run Jones! Run Jones!

SIXTEEN

Third Period prep, Friday, I was putting the finishing touches on my daily lesson plans for next week, and, for that matter, suggestions for the rest of the year, in case my sub, whoever that might be, gave a hang. Maddog McDermutt had phoned Tuesday night; I would fly to the Black Hills; this was my last day of school. Maddog would pick me up at the Rapid City Airport on a 2:30 Sunday arrival. Then directly to the kennels. Schooling races began Monday. I had to make proper arrangements with the track; all the boys would contribute dogs to my kennel. Maddog said they had my dogs picked out already. I would have to learn thirty dogs' names in a hurry. And their weights. Maddog said it might take a good week to ease into the routine; accordingly, he suggested that Sally, Jones, Fard, Miss Neopolitan and her pups drive over in the truck on the next weekend.

And I agreed.

The counselor, what's-her-name, blew in. "The janitors can't find <u>Of Mice and Men</u>," she said.

"That's understandable," I said. "I hid them."

"Well, where are they? The school board intends to ban

that book."

I took the fifth by shrugging. She huffed off.

I hadn't been paying much attention to Harry and Sheldon; they were babbling on again about their hunting dogs, something about field trials up on the highline somewhere. The principal came in, started his campfire.

"Hi," I said.

He blew smoke all over the place, then said: "I plan to observe you Monday, First Period. Don't do anything special. Be yourself. Most first year teachers panic on administrative observations. Simply follow your lesson plans. And wear a tie."

Harry and Sheldon were looking at me.

I tore out four pages of lesson plans and shoved them across the table to Dr. Mayonaisse.

The principal looked them over. "I love prepared teachers," he said, glancing at Sheldon and Harry.

"Dr. Mayonaisse," I said, "have you ever read Of Mice and Men?" The principal looked at me. "I can't recall. Is it a biology reference?"

"I'm sure you will enjoy my class, Dr. Mayonaisse," I said, shoving back my chair which squeaked marvelously.

"Give 'em what for in Rapid, McNulty," Sheldon said.

"We'll be watching the newspaper for track records out of that Jones fella," Harry said.

"Yeah," Sheldon added. "If you can get him to run the right way."

"Jones is coming over in a couple of weeks," I explained. "He'll be driving over with my wife and Fard Worthington from Ulm, and Fard's litter of pups. Maddog thought it would be best for me to get straightened around with the general kennel, before I took on green pups. You'll be hearing about Down Under Jones. I guarantee it."

I paused at the door. I grinned. I asked Dr. Mayonaisse. "Sir, do you have a dog?"

"No. Why do you ask?"

"Well, an educator who doesn't have a dog I think is missing something."

"It is a matter worthy of serious consideration," Dr. Mayonaisse said. "Have there been any studies on the subject?"

Had I just found a home for the chow chows? "I'm outta here," I said.

A few days later, under the strict tutelage of the master dog trainer Maddog McDermutt, I, school teacher Ryan McNulty, had learned the following about Rapid City dog track life: sleep four hours and work twenty. Why was I surprised? It was just like Key West. Then, when you're done with everything, what remains is your reward: the infamous Rapid City kennel cough, a devious virus that makes the dogs hack and dry heave and doesn't quite kill them. It's a lot of fun to have a racing kennel that can't race. According to Maddog and the boys, the kennel sickness takes about a week to run its course, another week to bring the dogs back into condition and on their weights. "What do you do with them in the meantime?" I asked.

Fleas Finnegan said: "Feed 'em. If they'll eat."

Ben Dover added: "Listen to 'em cough."

"Well, why aren't your dogs sick?" I asked.

Maddog, Hugh Mungas, and Little Elsie walked down to

the rail, laden down with racing programs, pop, and bags of popcorn. "Well, who do we like in The First?" Maddog asked.

"I'm partial to that Six dog," Fleas said.

Mangy Martinez, Dogbreath Smith arrived railside. "Nah," Dogbreath said, "that Six fades. All break and fade. Watch that Two dog."

I wasn't much interested. I couldn't have bet even if I wanted to. All I had left was change in my pants pocket which I had been saving to make an emergency phone call if it came to that.

In spite of the kennel cough setback, I was excited about the whole thing. I don't know why. I guess because it was different. For one thing I didn't have to make out lesson plans, almost worth it for that reason alone. I had thirty dogs in the kennel, leaving plenty of room for Jones, Miss Neopolitan and the pups when they arrived with Sally and Fard day after tomorrow.

And, I had learned a great deal.

A few days ago, for example, Ben Dover taught me how to worm thirty dogs. "Blow em out," Ben said. Begin with prune juice, milk of magnesia, and mineral oil. Loosen 'em up a bit." Then I helped Ben administer pills: big, stinky ones, and then Ben's dogs' eyes kind of rolled around, and they burped all morning. Ben said the trick was to kill the worms, not the dogs; Ben said Mangy Martinez murdered his whole kennel three years ago by overworming, although everybody seemed to have the theory his dogs had a new kind of worm that lived in the vital organs. Anyway, a couple of hours later, here comes Dr. Ben Dover again with his prune juice, milk of magnesia, and mineral oil, and "Blow 'em out" was literal. The dogs blew worms clean across the yard. We were very successful with round worms, tape worms, hook, and a few other things I did not recognize. Ben said, "When your dogs get over the kennel cough, give 'em a few days, then worm 'em."

I also learned how to collect, shred, trade over, and dispose of paper. Dogs sleep in shredded newspapers, shredded because I shredded it. Down one side one day, next side the next, and so on, fresh bedding. The dogs appreciated it. It was comforting to listen to a dog make a new nest, sniff, adjust the paper, dig around, fluff it up, circle and circle, then contentedly lie down to rest, a big sigh of satisfaction. I wished they would all stop hacking. And, I was worried about the kennel's bills, and I said so:

"Maddog," I said, "how do I make any money if all my dogs are sick and can't run?"

"You don't. You wait it out."

"Well how come all my dogs are sick and none of yours are sick?"

Once again no volunteers rushed to answer my question.

"I seem to be short, Maddog. I paid my kennel rent. I paid my meat bill. I paid my dry food bill. I only have change left."

After a moment, Maddog said, "Well boys, are we going to bet THE FIRST?"

I cleared my throat. "Furthermore, what do I eat on?" I asked. "I can't make it without money."

Hugh Mungas said. "You won't starve. Look at us. We've been running on empty for years, right?"

"Right," they all chorused.

197

I pulled my change out and looked at it. I could always call home, collect, and have Sally wire me some money. That, however, was an admission of failure.

Fleas said, "How about I buy you a hot-dog?"

"Really?" I said. "You mean it?" I was starved.

"Sure. Mustard? Pickles?"

"The works," I said. "And thanks."

"Don't mention it," Fleas said, and he moseyed off to buy me a hot-dog.

"That was nice," I said to anybody who cared to hear.

"We'd better make up our minds if we're going to bet this here First Race," Maddog said.

"I miss Jones," I said. "He could win three Grade A races a week. That'd help pay the bills."

"Speaking of your dog Jones," Maddog said, "I'm afraid I have some bad news." Maddog pulled a piece of paper from an inside pocket of his pink jump suit.

"Bad news?" I said. I was ready to punch his lights out if he was going to tell me he couldn't find Jones' papers.

Maddog read aloud.

Dear Maddog:

Mom is going to sell the pups and Miss Neopolitan to research. I realize we were to ride to Rapid City with Mrs. McNulty, but under the circumstances, that's impossible. We had to vanish. See you in Rapid City. Jones has joined us.

Sincerely,

Fard Worthington.

I had something to ask: "Why is Jones with Fard Worthington?"

IT IS NOW POST TIME

The crowd, about five hundred fans, settled down for the start of the first race.

THEY'RE OFF!!!!

Absently, I watched eight racing Greyhounds thunder by, dirt flying behind them, around the first turn, a couple swinging wide, then by the tote board, and I forgot about them.

Why is Jones with Fard Worthington?

First of all I come all the way to Rapid City on good faith. I quit a good job to do it, a job with a paycheck at the end of the month. I spend all my finances buying these free lunch artists meals, and now all my dogs are in the kennels wretching their guts up, with a kennel cough the boys say takes a week to run its course, provided the dogs live through it.

Why aren't any of their dogs sick?

199

And now I learn my dog Jones, the main reason I came to the track in the first place, to prove to the world he could really run like the wind, my dog, MY DOG, vanishes? Where in the hell is my dog?

"Where in the hell is my dog!" I shouted.

"It'll be nice to see Fard," Maddog said. "I should have bet that Five dog. Well then, let's not miss out on The Second Race."

"What do you mean, it'll be nice to see Fard?"

Maddog said, "He said he'd see us in Rapid City."

I thought about it.

"I suppose he's going to walk," I said.

"More or less would be my guess," Maddog said.

"It's 550 miles by road," I said. "A small overnight hike?"

"You have a point there," Maddog said. "I'm thinking on it."

I left Maddog McDermutt to think, if that's what you could call it, for a phone booth to spend my change; if I called collect on a pay phone, the pay phone should spit it back.

I dropped in my change and dialed home.

Sally answered, accepted my collect call. The pay phone went ding ding. I waited.

"Hello?" Sally said.

"Hello!" I said. I banged on the phone.

"Hello?"

"Hello!" Nothing. No change. The thing ate my money. "Where's Jones?" I demanded.

"I don't know," Sally said. "I let him out two days ago for his constitutional, and he never came back. He misses you. I think he went out to Fard's, looking for you. I've been trying to call you."

"Allow me to inform you. It's against the law to have a

phone in the kennel. Secondly, it appears that Jones is with Fard Worthington. That old drunken sot Mrs. Worthington sold the pups and Miss Neopolitan to research. And maybe Jones."

"That's awful," Sally said. "What can I do?"

"That stupid Jones," I said, "is liable to end up on some quack's dissecting table for bone and joint research. I need some money, Dear. My kennel is sick. Could you wire me a couple hundred?"

"I suppose so."

"Use Western Union. No. Never mind. Hop in the truck, go to the bank, withdraw a couple of hundred, and drive for here."

An operator cut in, said: "Please deposit twenty cents for an additional three minutes."

I quickly said, "I miss you and I need your help. Bye."

I joined the trainers at railside. Fleas handed me a hot-dog, and although cold, I ate it.

I leaned against the rail, wondering where my Greyhound was. With precocious Fardington Worthington? Well then, where was he? Maddog rubbed his chin, flicked something off the front of his pink jump suit, and said, "I have seen the light."

I continued to lean against the rail for some time, watching several races go by, and Maddog McDermutt think. Neither experience was very exciting. As for me, I saw no light whatsoever.

"Boys," Maddog finally said, "I think I know what Fard is up to. We're gonna do us some public relations work. Little Elsie, pencil and paper, you're the secretary. Fleas, Ben, Hugh, Mangy, here's what I want you fellas to do."

SEVENTEEN

Time for celebration. After two weeks of frustrating kennel cough, I finally had my dogs schooled in. Sally and I had four entries in for this evening's card; the First Race concluded, moments ago, and we breathlessly awaited the results.

The tote board lit up.

"Yes!" I said. "Yes! We did it." I gave my wife a big hug. It became a back-slapping, happy occasion. We did it. After two weeks, we really did it. Everybody loved a winner.

Sally asked Fleas: "How much is a fourth place worth?"

Fleas thought about it. "Oh...about $3.80"

"$3.80?" Sally asked.

"Something like that. Depends on last week's handle."

"I see. Well that hardly pays the bills, does it?"

"We have three more in tonight," I said. "I think they'll do well."

THE DOGS ARE ON THE TRACK
FOR THE SECOND RACE

"Anybody seen Maddog?" I asked.

Pooch the Mooch said, "He's around here somewhere." I've never seen a guy so busy. On the phone all the time.

203

Radio. Television. Newspapers. Magazines. Maddog doesn't miss a bet. He's in his element."

Fleas said, "Here comes the man of the hour now."

Maddog had a large grin on his kisser. "Good news, folks. Really good news. We have a note from Fard."

"Well hurry up and let's have it," Hugh Mungas said. "It's been two weeks."

"Well, if you let me read it, then you'll know," Maddog said.

So we all listened.

Dear Maddog:

Sorry we did not make Rapid City for opening night. I am writing this note from an island on the Missouri where we have been hiding out. I have taken the opportunity to work with the dogs daily. I plan to float the Missouri River to Fort Peck, then drive the team to Rapid, by back roads and cross country. I shall call you when I can. Looking forward to seeing you all.

Fard Worthington.

P.S. Tell Mr. McNulty Jones is fine. He is our lead dog. He'll get us there.

Maddog said, "I was right."

"Maddog," Fleas said, "how does Fard write us a letter

from an island in the Missouri?"

"Well, he probably mailed it from a town along the way."

"Do you have the postmark on the envelope?" I asked.

Maddog looked the envelope over, said, "Virgelle?"

"Below Loma," I said. "Missouri flows east after Virgelle. I'll be darned. He's moving east on the Missouri."

Sally said, "He's coming to Rapid City on that dog sled?"

I said to Sally: "Well, in that case, of course Jones would be the lead dog."

Sally nodded. "Of course," she said.

"Shhh," Maddog shushed. "There's another postscript."

P.S.S. Also, tell Mr. McNulty the English teacher
I am keeping an extensive diary. I plan to write a
book about the trip.

"That sounds fun," I said.

Nobody paid much attention to the dogs for the Second Race, now out on the track.

IT IS NOW POST TIME

We paused to watch the lure speed up down the back stretch and bounce and spark its way around the far turn. The starting boxes crashed open, and eight racing Greyhounds lunged out and thundered by.

"I forget," I said to Sally, "did we have a dog in the Second?"

"Number Seven," she said.

"Seven?" Where was Seven. Oh there he was.

"Seven?"

"Seven."

I watched Seven run around the first turn, by the tote board, around the far turn and head for home, by the finish line and to the curtain where the lead-out boys ran out and collared and leashed up the racers. If I was not mistaken, Seven ran seventh.

"Well, he beat one dog," Sally said.

"There goes our streak," I said.

As the evening wore on, our third racer took a very solid sixth place, and our forth and last entry in the Tenth Race ran dead last.

Back at the kennel Sally advised me that she would never complain about teacher salaries again, if she lived to be seven hundred years old.

Three days passed before another word from Fard. We were once again gathered railside, munching popcorn, sipping cokes; one of the guys once in awhile bet a dog. Last night our kennel knocked 'em dead. We won three races, a maiden, an E, and a D, and were in the money three other times, two thirds and a forth, and only had six entries. Six for six in the money. Sally had added it up. $144, more or less, depending on the handle. Once in awhile somebody would say, "It'd sure be nice if we heard from Fard." Or, "I sure hope Fard's all right." Or, "I wonder how that Fard is getting along." Or, "I wonder where they're camping tonight."

Between the Fifth and Sixth races, we all heard the following announcement over the public address system.

LONG DISTANCE CALL FOR MADDOG MCDERMUTT. MADDOG MCDERMUTT PLEASE REPORT TO THE RACING SECRETARY'S OFFICE ABOVE THE CLUBHOUSE.

206

"Well," Maddog said, adjusting his Vote Republican button. "Guess who."

So we all grinned and elbowed each other because we knew very well guess who.

"Ask him how Jones is!" I yelled at Maddog's back as he waddled off through the crowd.

We watched the Sixth and Seventh races go by before Maddog returned.

"Well?" Fleas demanded.

"This is even better than I'd hoped for," Maddog said, cracking his knuckles.

"Are Fard and the dogs all right?" Sally asked.

"What about Jones?" I wanted to know.

Maddog leaned on the rail, looked out at the tote, to the first turn, to the far turn, then said to all of us: "They're fine. They went cross-country to begin with, headed west, cut across the Sun River watershed, crossed the Sun between Vaughn and the town of Sun River, followed I-15 about twenty miles to the west, spent two days and nights in a Hutterite Colony where, once Fard told the Hoots the problem, they pitched right in with eight tractor tire inner tubes, four sheets of plywood with drilled holes in 'em, and rope. Middle of the night Fard and the dogs lit out for the Missouri River, crossed I-15 in the dark, spent a week on an island somewhere between Carter and Fort Benton, stocked up on fish, caught suckers and carp with maggots, then turned around and used the suckers and carp to catch sturgeon and catfish on setlines at night. Fard smoked everything. Says he has enough smoked fish to make Rapid."

"Where'd he call from?" I asked.

"Robinson Bridge," Maddog said.

I knew Robinson Bridge. Fard was almost to the headwaters of Fort Peck. "Floating the sled on tractor tubes, you say?"

"That's the word," Maddog said.

"Ingenious," Pooch the Mooch McGill said.

"Bravo, Fard," Hugh Mungas said. "Bravo."

"Did he mention Jones?" I asked.

"All the kid could do was rave on about Jones, how strong he was, what a great leader. How hard he pulled. How well he followed instructions."

Jones?

"I had to cut the call short," Maddog explained. "It was collect. He did add one thing, but if I were you I wouldn't brag on it, because it's out of season, you know. Jones and that wolf apparently tired of fish. Somewhere below Virgelle the two of 'em took a pretty good-sized buck up a coulee, up and ran him down for dinner, and so everybody for the last two days has been on meat."

I glanced at Sally, then said to Maddog, "Jones caught a deer?"

"No," Maddog said. "Not a deer. An antelope. A full grown buck antelope."

"Wow," I said. "Holy wow! Maddog, do you know what that means?"

"I know what that means," Maddog said. "I know very well what that means."

IT IS NOW POST TIME

The Tenth Race went by, the Three dog in front by a length. "Look," Sally said, "that Number Three is our dog. I think we're going to win this one."

And we did. Three won by four lengths. We took fifth in

the Eleventh Race and a second in the Twelfth. By golly, we had a racing kennel on our hands. We were actually competitive. We were starting to gain a little respect. In the overall kennel standings we were slowly catching up to the next-to-the-last kennel operated by Pooch the Mooch McGill. I pointed that out to him. Pooch said all his dogs had kennel cough. "That's a shame," I said.

The next day we gathered at railside for the First Race where we were met by a reporter from a Rapid City newspaper. The reporter wanted to know where he could find Maddog McDermutt. Within ten minutes two radio stations and two television crews, all from Rapid City, arrived to interview Maddog McDermutt.

The man of the hour arrived with a grand, sweeping gesture of his right hand, for no particular reason except perhaps he was an ex drama minor, and said, "Well, what a we got here?" I wished he had washed his pink jump suit or worn something else.

He stood at the rail, something like Napoleon, hand over his stomach, head thrown back, looking out over the dog track.

"We understand there is a litter of Greyhound pups coming to Rapid City in a unique way. Mr. McDermutt, could you tell us about it?"

Maddog grunted, then faced the cameras, said. "I'd be glad to. My Godson, Fardington Maddog Worthington, is bringing a litter of Greyhound pups to Rapid City from Great Falls."

"Montana?"

"Yes. Great Falls, Montana. The last time we heard from Fard was from the Robinson Bridge on the Missouri River."

MONTANA

FORT BENTON

VAUGHN

MISSOURI RIVER

ULM · GREAT FALLS

WYOMIN

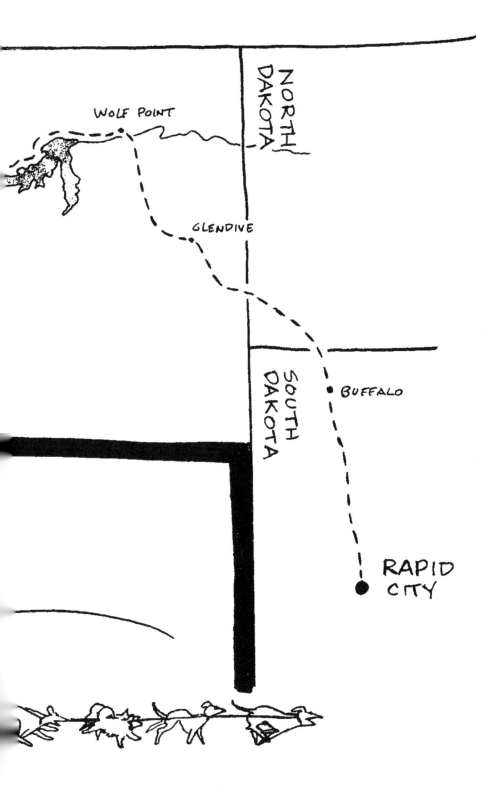

LONG DISTANCE CALL FOR MADDOG MCDERMUTT. MADDOG MCDERMUTT PLEASE REPORT TO THE RACING SECRETARY'S OFFICE ABOVE THE CLUBHOUSE.

"Excuse me," Maddog said. "I have a long distance phone call. Talk to the English teacher there. His dog is the lead dog."

A newscaster, turning to me, said, "Your dog is leading the team?" He shoved a mike in my face.

"Well that's my understanding."

"What's your dog's name?" the newscaster asked.

"Jones. Down Under Jones. He's Australian."

"What is the relationship of your dog to the boy and his dogs?"

"You'll have to talk to Maddog," I said. "Maddog McDermutt is handling all the public relations details."

Another newscaster asked Fleas, "I understand there is a wolf on the team."

Another wanted to know: "Greyhounds pulling a dog sled? Isn't that unusual? Don't huskies pull dog sleds? Maddog McDermutt mentioned a couple of chow chows on the team. And what about the wolf? A real wolf?"

The questions continued; cameras pointed; pencils scratched on pads. Maddog was back. "They're in North Dakota," he said. "And moving south."

"Everybody's OK?" I asked.

"Everybody's OK," Maddog said. "They're on the way."

"How many days before their arrival?" A newscaster asked.

212

Maddog turned, smiled into the camera, "I think about a week," he said. "Let's plan on Saturday afternoon, downtown Rapid City, 12 noon sharp. And if you fellas would come on over here, I'll give you all the details."

EIGHTEEN

Saturday. 11:45. Downtown Rapid City, South Dakota. Sally, and I, and the dog trainers, stood along the curb of St. Joseph Street, along with thousands of others. Maddog McDermutt had gone crazy on this one. Rapid City was his. All his.

All week long Maddog had been busy with the various news media. Once the story broke in Rapid City, it was front page news all the way, every day, the story of the boy from Montana, somewhere between Great Falls and Rapid City, with a mixed litter of dogs that he was protecting from scientific bone and joint experimentation or pickled cadavers for veterinarian undergraduates, and it wasn't long before the national news people glommed on.

Fard was front page material. Day after day the headlines hit the streets:

BOY, WOLF, GREYHOUNDS
ON WAY TO BLACK HILLS

WOLF AND DOG TEAM
CROSS MONTANA BORDER

FARD WORTHINGTON FIVE DAYS FROM RAPID

FARD WORTHINGTON MUSHING TO RAPID

DOG TEAM CROSSES SOUTH DAKOTA BORDER

FARD TWO DAYS FROM RAPID

MONTANA DOGS AND WOLF
ARRIVE RAPID NOON TODAY

All the Rapid City radio stations were hot with the story, fed to them by the last of the great public relations masterminds: Maddog McDermutt. It was my feeling Maddog had not actually heard from Fard in the last three days; he said Fard was constantly in touch, but I doubted it; I don't see how that was possible. If our information as to their route was correct, Fard and the dogs were going through some mighty wild country. Maddog, I suspect, filled in the blanks for the press. He confided in me once, said if those guys don't have any news, you'll notice, they make it up. On dull days they end up interviewing each other, or they do the news negatively, like nothing happened in this regard or in such and such and soon you're worried about that nothing that didn't happen and pretty soon that nothing becomes something .... and I think I followed that. I do know, however, that Maddog and Fard had planned for a noon downtown finale. That much

I knew.

The Rapid City press, we all came to find out, was but a warmup exercise for the likes of Maddog McDermutt.

Maddog had lured the major news networks to town. I had seen today in various locations, signs of ABC, CBS, NBC, down by the first turn of the dog track, out along the road, on top of the grandstands. Camera crews had popped up like sprouting mushrooms all over the place. I had seen the a blimp drifting north several hours ago.

We had good positions in front of the Alex Johnson Hotel. It was a good thing we had come early, because St. Joseph was lined with people, the crowd now five, six, seven people deep, some sitting on the curbs, some kids riding their fathers' shoulders for a better look, vendors taking advantage of the situation, selling balloons, popcorn, cotton candy, soft drinks, ice cream. It had become a circus, and center ring was Maddog McDermutt.

"I didn't know so many people lived here," Sally commented.

"There's a mess of em," Fleas said.

Maddog came down the street, clipboard in hand. He ticked off a few items, then looked up, said: "Lovely day for a parade, eh folks?"

We all agreed with that.

We heard a siren in the distance.

"That would be my godson Fard now," Maddog said.

We all looked down St. Joseph but could not see anything yet. "They'll make the corner down there at Sixth," Maddog said. "That's the route. That's the plan."

The siren went off again. Closer.

The crowd grew expectant, everybody leaning into the moment. We could hear the racket around the corner: motorcycles, cars, trucks, the crowd applauding, everything moving closer to the corner of Sixth and St. Joseph. The blimp floated above the tops of the buildings.

Two motorcycle policemen cleared the corner first, one on each side of the street, making a wide arch to keep the crowd back on the sidewalks. One of the sirens went off. Two more motorcycle policemen followed. The motorcycles moved down St. Joseph in our direction, two policemen on each side of the street. A big flatbed truck drove around the corner, television crew and cameras on board. The blimp turned, floated over the corner, no doubt filming the approach of what we could not yet see from the street. Another truck came around the corner, another film crew. Photographers were running along, ready to take pictures.

"I hear 'em," Hugh said, and the minute he said it, I could hear it too: the excited yapping of dogs above the yells, and cheers, the applause of the crowd, the hum of the blimp engines, the hum of the motorcycles going by; folks were pointing, craning necks, and then there they were, rounding the corner of Sixth and St. Joseph, and in front, the lead dog, a great brindled Greyhound, Jones, my Jones, Down Under Jones, leaning in to the traces, powerful shoulder and back muscles bulging, chest heaving, tongue hanging out, mouth frothing, Miss Neopolitan behind him, pulling equally as hard, leaning into the traces, the two chow chows, and the five Greyhound pups, no these weren't pups anymore, they were dogs, all of them yapping, and to the rear of the sled, Fardington Maddog Worthington. The wolf. I did not see the

218

wolf. The wolf was not with the team. And Fard, Mr. Western himself: Stetson, Levis jacket, leather belt with the huge buckle F.A.R.D., Levis pants, pointy cowboy boots. Fard waved to the crowd, and the crowd waved back and cheered.

"Atta boy, Fard." "You show 'em, Fard." "We're with ya, Fard." "Go get 'em Fard."

And then I saw him, drifting wide on the corner, running along easily, riding shotgun as it were, off to the left, for some reason not in harness, the wolf. I think he was bigger than Jones. He was magnificent. He was moving with the sled, floating along, off Fard's left shoulder. For a moment the sun caught his yellow eyes. Bystanders saw him, moved back, gave him plenty of room; even the ones who acted belligerent with the motorcycle policemen squeezed back, back, back, let the wolf go by. When the team was directly in front of us I hollered: "Jones!"

The ears went up. He heard me. "Jones!" I yelled again, and the tail went up and the ears went down, then up again, and he lunged, and the sled jerked forward, then ground to a stop, and I had a big Greyhound in my face; Jones had his front paws on my shoulders, licking my face, and I did not mind. "Jones," I babbled, "you silly ass. Golly, I'm glad to see you." And I hugged him, and he washed my face some more, and I hugged him some more, and he whined, and he barked in my ear, then barked at Fard, then he saw Sally and gave her the treatment, washed her face stem to stern, and she hugged him and told him we were glad he was all right, and finally Jones dropped to all fours, shook himself, looked at Fleas who put his hands up and said.... "I'd rather not...," then Jones looked back at Fardington, like well we've come this far, let's get the rest of it over with.

Maddog said, "Dog track's about twelve miles, Fard. Mind if we walk along for awhile?"

And Jones looked at me, as if to say, it's OK, we'll get together later, and I said, "Good job, old buddy." And he was at my face again, legs over my shoulders, and I was laughing, and hugging him.

"I think they're in love," Maddog McDermutt said, and then he leaned over and whispered in my ear, "the national networks are filming this."

"So what?" I said.

I looked at him.

"Well that sort of thing is a little embarrassing," he said.

"All right, Jones," I said. "Back to work. Twelve more miles. After 700 miles cross-country I guess you can make twelve more down a paved road."

And we joined in, half of us on one side, and the rest on the other side, all of us taking turns petting this dog and that dog, and we moved on down St. Joseph. The wolf pup came up alongside, and I patted him. Maddog moved as if with purpose, as if his destiny was upon him. "Look at the muscles on the backs of those dogs," Pooch the Mooch said to Fleas. "These dogs are in shape."

Fleas nodded. "They look great," he said. He reached over to pat a chow on the neck.

"We've been eating a lot of fish," Fard said. "It's good for them."

The wolf moved up to the front of the sled to walk along with Jones, shoulder to shoulder, and I wondered what I was worried about. I could not imagine what those two could not handle. They sniffed noses, bumped shoulders, tails wagging, tongues lolling out, chests heaving, ears perked, the sled moving on down St. Joseph, the long journey nearly at an end. As if to accentuate my thought, a hunting dog, I'll say a golden lab, or something like that, stood in the middle of the road and watched the team come down the road. He moved to his left, a step or two, as if he was not sure of what he saw. When he had it in mind that coming down the road at him were ten critters with purpose, Jones and the wolf right up front, he decided that he wanted no part of it and hightailed it up an alley. I couldn't blame him.

The crowd lining the streets thinned out as we moved away from the center of town.

"Maddog," Fleas said, "I hope you took into consideration we are still twelve miles from the dog track."

"Indeed I did, indeed I did," Maddog said, flagging a flatbed truck alongside. We all piled on.

"Hey Fard!" Maddog yelled. "Let's see what that bunch can do."

Fard turned.

"Straight ahead, Fard!" Maddog yelled. "Less than twelve miles. What a ya say, let's see those guys motivate." Maddog waved at the blimp.

Fard straightened up, tipped his hat, hollered: "Let's go! Hiieee! Go Jones! Go team! Mush!"

Jones lunged, dug in. The pups and Miss Neopolitan dug in. And the dog sled picked up speed. All the dogs were yapping.

Maddog looked in the cab of the truck. "By golly they're doing almost twenty!" He said.

221

A truck marked CBS pulled alongside, cameras pointed at Fard and the team. On the other side NBC cranked away.

"We're gonna make the cover of TIME," Maddog said.

In no time at all we hit Highway 92, turned, and the dog sled moved right on, our truck directly behind, the camera crews maintaining position, the motorcycle policemen out front alerting oncoming traffic, and at least a mile of cars and trucks following.

Sally said, "I'll bet you really miss the class room now."

Maddog asked no one in particular: "How long do you think it'd take that bunch to cover 1,000 miles?"

"They just went about 700, didn't they?" I said.

"I believe that's a safe estimate," Maddog said. "They were taking their time. They could have been here three days ago. But how about in snow and ice and temperatures way below zero?"

"Those Greyhounds don't have much for hairy coats, Maddog," Fleas said.

"You ever hear of sweaters?" Maddog said. "And booties?"

We settled back on the flatbed truck to watch the team work.

They were beautiful. Simply magnificent. No yapping now. The team was at a gallop. Like Maddog, I wondered how long they could keep it up. And Jones, out in front.

"Track's right up ahead, Fard!" Little Elsie yelled. "Turn right, go on down the dirt road, come in the back gate, once around the track, then stop at the finish line. Right, Maddog?"

Maddog noted something on his clipboard. "Right," he said.

Fard waved. I waved. He grinned. He slowed the yapping dogs to a walk to turn off the highway.

And around the corner everybody went, Jones leading the way, down the dirt road, circled around behind the dog track, and in the side gate, and we were going down the Rapid City Dog Track, past the starting boxes, to a standing room only crowd. I doubt there ever was a crowd like this for any dog race, anywhere. Entrepreneur extraordinare Maddog McDermutt at work. Maddog waved at the standing room only crowd.

"Mush!" Fard yelled, stepping up onto the sled's railings. "Mush!"

And Jones lowered his head, humped up his shoulders, dug his nails in, lunged forward, all the dogs lunged forward, and the sled burst ahead, past the finish line. We all stood up on the back of the truck bed to watch them go around; the crowd came to life with a roar. This was the show Maddog the ex drama minor had written. This was what the crowd had been waiting to see. Fard Worthington and his dog sled approached the first turn full steam ahead, throttle to the floor, pedal to the metal, and that big dog in front wasn't swinging wide on this one, no sir; he leaned into it, and the team leaned into it, and I tell you that dog sled was moving, that dog sled was really moving, coming off the first turn and headed down the backstretch. "Is that the Great Falls reject you boys claimed couldn't run the first turn?" I yelled. "I told you that dog can run. Go Jones!" I yelled. "Run Jones!"

And the wolf, who had been running at the side of the sled, made a move in about six great floating strides, and eased up alongside Jones.

I glanced up at the blimp, hovering over the dog track.

"Remind me to call The Biscayne Irish American Derby and The Flagler International Derby!" Maddog yelled. "We have to enter that big boy in those Derbies."

"The $40,000 Biscayne Irish American," Ben Dover said. "That's more money than a guy would know what to do with."

"Look at that Greyhound lead that team," Maddog said. "That, boys, is a Greyhound, that's what that is."

"That's my Greyhound," I said.

"That's our Greyhound," Maddog said.

The looks from the dog trainers were pathetic. Maddog leaned over and hissed in my ear: "You want to take the heart right out of it?"

Sally said, "It won't hurt anything."

"Right," I said. "I stand corrected. Our dog."

"Go Jones!" Hugh Mungas yelled.

"Run Jones!" Ben Dover yelled.

And we all joined in. "Run Jones! Run Jones! Run Jones!" *You, me, the dog.*

Around the far turn I watched the dog sled sail along, round the far turn, head for the finish line, slow.

The dog sled came to a stop at the finish line, and I jumped off the flatbed truck to give my panting, heaving dog a big hug. His giant rib cage heaved; his eyes rolled back; he looked like he was laughing. "You're some kind of dog, Jones," I said. I moved down the line, patted Miss Neopolitan, then the Greyhound pups. I patted the two chow chows. "You guys are something else," I said.

The wolf pup came alongside for a pat and I gave him a hug.

And now the politics: the track manager and the racing secretary, handshakes all around and congratulations and isn't life wonderful, and all the while the television cameras recording everything, and now out of the crowd and onto the track come some guys in fur parkas, no doubt checking out the competition, and they shake everybody's hand, and now the dog food people, and I think Maddog could hear the cash registers dinging, and somebody said a producer from Hollywood with two screenwriters were snooping around, and the man in the pink jump suit, granny glasses, Stetson, Siberian ski boots, VOTE REPUBLICAN button, was in the middle of it all, and I guess maybe he did minor in drama after all, and a boy came up to tell Maddog he had a phone call from Portland where the track manager wondered if he would like to enter Jones in the Multnomah Derby, and Maddog told the boy, not right now, that he would return the call, and all the while the crowd watching. It was over.

Almost.

Maddog stepped up to the mike. We all quieted down.

"Ladies and Gentlemen," he said. "I am pleased to introduce to you my godson Fardington Maddog Worthington and his team of dogs from Great Falls, Montana."

Maddog waited for the crowd to quiet down again.

"It is my pleasure to announce that we are going into negotiations with a dog food company, to sponsor Fardington Maddog Worthington in some dog sled races. Additionally, my godson, Fard Worthington, has kept a diary of his adventures, and as his agent I can assure you his story would make a great book and movie."

Maddog drew me aside. "You still think that big fella is

225

the fastest dog in the world?"

"Maddog," I said, "I'm an English teacher. I am full of hyperbole."

"No," he said. "You're a dog trainer. I've seen it. All the boys and Little Elsie have seen it. You found run in dogs that had been sick a week quicker than any of the rest of us would. Now answer the question: what about that Jones fella?"

For some reason, I glanced at the finish line rail. I blinked. Harry Ringling and Sheldon Adamson were standing there, taking it all in, grinning. I waved. They waved back. "Just a minute, Maddog," I said, rushing over to the rail. "What are you guys doing here?"

Harry spoke for the both of them: "Your dog has been front page news all week long. We wouldn't have missed this show for anything."

"Golly, it's great to see you."

"You missed your interview with Dr. Mayonaisse."

"What do you mean?"

"Well, he observed your class. That's always followed by an interview."

"What'd he do, observe my sub?"

"You got it."

"Well, I hope I did all right. How's Bobo?" I asked.

"Fine," Sheldon said.

"And Monty?"

"Couldn't be better," Harry said.

Sheldon said, "Your English students missed you."

"Really?" I said. I thought about it. "Really?"

Harry was looking at Jones. "When's that big dumb mutt you call a dog gonna take a turn?"

226

Sheldon chipped in. "Yeah. We came 550 miles to see the last of the great pheasant dogs run around a dog track."

"And that you shall," I said. "That you shall." I trotted back to Maddog.

"Maddog," I said, "let's do it."

Maddog returned to the mike. "Ladies and Gentlemen. We have one more surprise. You will notice this dog sled has a leader, an extremely large Greyhound, and his name is.....Jones. Down Under Jones." Maddog paused, muffled the mike with his hand, said to me, "Unclip that harness. Push the dog sled into the infield there."

Fard helped me take the harness off Jones. I put my arm around Jones, gave him a hug, whispered in his ear, "they want to see you run." I released my hold on Jones; he wandered over to the finish line where he saluted the photo finish mirrors. The crowd applauded mildly. The wolf followed, sniffed, and he too saluted the mirrors. The crowd applauded again. Maddog was back to the mike, in full control, in his element. "Ladies and gentlemen!"

Maddog stepped back, yet another pause, and turned to me: "Hand school him, don't put him in the box. Take him down to the starting boxes, and we'll get that rabbit rolling." Maddog waved to the camera crews and the blimp.

I walked down the track. Jones walked along off to my side. The wolf pup followed Jones. Already the setup was screwy. You don't take a racing Greyhound to the starting boxes by calling him over. I didn't even have a leash. But Jones seemed agreeable. He trotted, amiably, caught up, stuck his nose in my hand, and I scratched his ear. When I reached the starting boxes, I crouched down in front of the Four Hole, grabbed him by the shoulders with one arm, and put my other arm around his stomach. If he became excited, I would lift his back feet off the ground. I looked down the track. The dog sled and Fard and Maddog and all the trainers and dignitaries had moved off the track into the infield. The crowd was starting to warm up again with cheers and applause. I whispered in Jones's ear: "Once around, Jones. No big deal." Jones licked my face. The lure was on the move. Jones's ears pricked straight up. He remembered!

"Come on, Jones," I said, giving him one last hug. "Let's see you crank it on. Remember Jacques Ra....beet, Jones. The stubble fields. The coulees. Do it for old Jacques." The mechanical rabbit rattled into the far turn. Maddog McDermutt was on the mike, yelling, his voice thundering all over the place: "Run Jones! Run Jones! Run Jones!" The special cheering section on the infield side of the finish line, Sally, eight dog trainers, Fard, and dignitaries joined in; Miss Neopolitan, two chow chows, and five Greyhound pups took on yapping and howling. The crowd joined in on Maddog's chant. "Run Jones! Run Jones! Run Jones!"

Another voice, off to my right, from beside the starting boxes, head tossed back, nose to the sky, chops wide open, adding to the clamor his two bits worth, and it sent a shiver down my spine: lonesome, ancient, timeless, yet here, here and now, and it shut everybody up in a hurry; the howl continued, lonely, sad, the cry of the wolf.

Jones's nails dug in. The mechanical rabbit rounded the turn, clattering and banging, bouncing and squawking. Jones heard it. Jones saw it. The wolf saw it, his howl gargling to a puzzled growl. I yelled "Go Jones!" and released him. Jones meant business, powerfully breaking free of my grip, and in three great strides Jones was flying down the track with acceleration that I had so many times seen out on the prairies. The first turn was coming up fast, and out of the corner of my eye I saw the wolf jump the rail and lope across the infield; the wolf planned to cut the rabbit off. The big Greyhound was almost on the lure. He leaned; he bore down; he dug in, reached out, stretched out, and I am here to tell you Jones took the paint off the rail. Maddog clasped both hands and raised them over his head, like he had just won the heavyweight championship of the world, by knock-out. Off the first turn and into the backstretch, and now that Jacques Ra....beet speed, those long ranging strides, so powerful he made it look easy, he was really moving, past the tote board; he had a look about him that he would have that lure, and he turned it on, found that other gear and Jones almost had that lure, he was but three feet from it, as the chant continued: "Run Jones!"

No other dog at this track could make a move like that.

Out of the corner of my eye I saw the wolf coming up on the infield side, beside Jones, and together they ran the far turn, neck and neck, Jones on the track, the wolf on the infield side, bearing down on the lure, and here was speed, and I knew it, and everybody in the place knew it, and I was afraid that if I didn't lose my dog to that idiot Maddog McDermutt's nutty scheme to run him in some silly dog sled race, then I would lose him to the derbies in Florida, and once again I was in over my head, from that night in Great Falls I put my arm around him, and took him home. I watched the dog and wolf thunder by, and I could not call his name; his name would not come to my lips; it was stuck in my throat.

Jones crossed the finish line; the wolf skirted the trainers and Fard and the pups, then jumped the rail, back on the track. The lure clattered into the trap. Jones came to a stop and looked at it and barked at it; the wolf came alongside Jones to stare at the fake; the wolf looked at Jones as if to say why we were chasing that?

"Let's put these guys away and feed 'em," Maddog said. "I, for one, have had quite a day."

"Amen," Little Elsie said.

"Amen," all the trainers said.

"Honors," I said. "Jones!"

"We wouldn't have it any other way," Maddog said, and everyone nodded.

We led the dog sled to the kennel compounds, and I opened the door to my kennel. Everybody filed in. We took the dogs from the traces and turned the team into the turnout yard.

Maddog looked them over.

"We keep them together, no matter what," he said. "That's only right. Well, we have our work cut out for us. We have the derbies to look forward to with that big dog; and I'll bet those pups run a pretty good lick or two; we have dog sled races; that ought to be good. They don't make the huskies can run with this bunch. We have television interviews; we have dog food sponsors and contracts; we have been approached by Hollywood; Fard's going to write a book; we tied a can to Greyhound research, at least for awhile; I think we are in good shape.

The Greyhounds in my kennel started in howling, a welcome to the newcomers. The dogs in the yard perked their ears, joined in. The kennel next door joined in. Then the kennels across the way, and in a moment we had 1000 dogs howling away, and the dogs in the yard joined in, and then, above the rest, louder, wilder, the howl of the wolf, sustained, above and beyond the howls of the other dogs, and the racket went on, and on, and we didn't even attempt to shut them up. I closed the kennel door; we all agreed to meet for coffee. I opened my truck door for Fard. I poked him on the arm as he climbed in.

"When do I read your diary?" I asked.

"Hey McNulty!" Maddog hollered from his truck window. "You want to invite these two school teachers along?"

I waved at Harry and Sheldon.

"Absolutely," I said.

Maddog drove by first. I pulled my truck into the line; we all caravaned past the security gate, down the back dirt road behind the dog track, up onto the highway, turned right, on to the bowling alley for coffee.